How to Select, Use & Maintain
Garden Equipment

P9-CFD-438

Created and
designed by the
editorial staff of
ORTHO Books

Written by
T. Jeff Williams

Illustrations by
Ron Hildebrand
Rik Olson

Designed by
Craig Bergquist
Christine Dunham

Cover photograph by
Fred Lyon

Ortho Books

Publisher
Robert L. Iacopi

Editorial Director
Min S. Yee

Managing Editor
Anne Coolman

Horticultural Editor
Michael D. Smith

Senior Editor
Kenneth R. Burke

Production Manager
Laurie S. Blackman

Horticulturist
Michael McKinley

Associate Editors
Barbara J. Ferguson
Susan M. Lammers

Production Assistant
Anne D. Pederson

Editorial Assistant
Julie W. Hall

Photo Librarian
Darcie S. Furlan

Copyediting by
Editcetera
Berkeley, CA

Typography by
Lehmann Graphics
Burlingame, CA

Graphic Production by
CABA Design Office
San Francisco, CA

Color Separations by
Color Tech
Redwood City, CA

Address all inquiries to:
Ortho Books
Chevron Chemical Company
Consumer Products Division
575 Market Street
San Francisco, CA 94105

Chevron Chemical Company
575 Market Street, San Francisco, CA 94105

Consultants

Gary Bender
Citrus Heights, CA

Dick Covert
Sacramento, CA

Remy Johnson
Horticulture Department
City College of San Francisco
San Francisco, CA

Denson Mott
Rio Linda, CA

Pat Stocking
San Anselmo, CA

Bob Vereen
National Retail
Hardware Association
Indianapolis, IN

Special Thanks to

Capel-Klang Companies
South San Francisco, CA

Ira and Ronnie Deitrick
Lafayette, CA

Ann Ludwig
San Francisco, CA

Mike Milanese
Pay Less Super Drug Stores
Oakland, CA

Pat Tompkins
San Mateo, CA

Mr. and Mrs. William G. Whelan
Lafayette, CA

Illustration Assistants

Ronda Hildebrand
Frank Hildebrand
Jeffrey Womble
Cyndie Clark-Huegel

Photographers

Fred Lyon: Front Cover, pages 4,
36, 62, 76, Back Cover—upper
right and left, lower right

Josephine Coatsworth: Back
Cover—lower left, pages 1, 6, 48

Michael McKinley: Page 37

Martin Schweitzer: Page 14

Cover Photograph

In just one corner of your garage
you can create a "garden center"
for storing and maintaining all your
garden equipment. See Chapter
One, page 12, for storage ideas.

Page One Photograph

Writer/Gardener T. Jeff Williams
maintains his gardening tools in
his light and airy workshop.
Throughout the book, he shows
you how to keep all your gardening
equipment in good condition.

How to Select, Use & Maintain
Garden Equipment

GARDEN EQUIPMENT BASICS

By following the guidelines in this chapter, you can select just the right tools for your gardening needs. Then, to ensure a long life for all your garden equipment, you'll learn the basics of proper use, storage, maintenance, and repair.

Olde axe

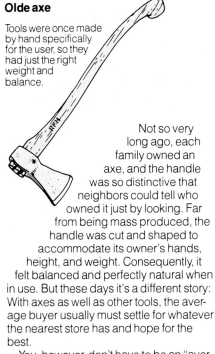

Tools were once made by hand specifically for the user, so they had just the right weight and balance.

Not so very long ago, each family owned an axe, and the handle was so distinctive that neighbors could tell who owned it just by looking. Far from being mass produced, the handle was cut and shaped to accommodate its owner's hands, height, and weight. Consequently, it felt balanced and perfectly natural when in use. But these days it's a different story: With axes as well as other tools, the average buyer usually must settle for whatever the nearest store has and hope for the best.

You, however, don't have to be an "average" buyer. You can explore the differences among various garden tools and end up with those that suit your particular requirements. Virtually all garden tools, from pruning shears to chainsaws, differ in quality of material, in workmanship, and in size. You can use this book to find out what will work best for you.

The modern gardener's garden equipment needs haven't really changed over

◀

Even simple tools require maintenance. Good care makes gardening fun for all.

the past 100 years: There are tools for preparing the ground for planting, and there are tools for keeping vegetables, flowers, or orchards free of weeds and disease.

This means that only a few tools are absolutely essential, but the actual number of tools available is staggering. These tools are designed to make gardening easier and more pleasurable, and many are well worth their cost in terms of time and energy saved. However, there is no point in wasting money on tools you don't really need—as you already know if you've ever purchased tools that looked irresistible in the store but lay unused in your tool shed. When you come across a tool you "just have to have," stop and evaluate your needs carefully: What is the tool's function? How often would you use it? Would a tool you already have do the job just as well? For example, there are many different types of hoes on the market, but do you need to own every one? For that matter, do you really need a hoe at all? The type and size of your garden are factors worth considering; it may be just as easy to do the weeding by hand.

Each section in this book will teach you about the purpose for which a tool was designed, and this knowledge will help you decide whether you really need the tool or not.

If you use a tool properly—that is, for its designated purpose and according to directions—it will stay in good condition for years. Misuse is one of the main reasons why tools get damaged and broken. Throughout this book, you will find helpful hints on the proper use of your tools.

What *is* misuse of tools? Well, suppose you throw your soil-encrusted shovel into a dark corner of the garage and consider

it stored. Thousands of gardeners do exactly this. But should it really come as a surprise when one day the shovel is so difficult to use that you're about ready to quit gardening? Yet it isn't hard to clean that shovel, sharpen those tools, and keep all your equipment in good working order. This book outlines the basic steps of garden equipment maintenance—from cleaning a trowel to trouble-shooting a gasoline engine that won't start. When you know the steps, good maintenance habits will come with practice.

Garden Equipment contains six chapters. The first covers general principles of tool and equipment selection, guidelines for maintenance, and storage and safety advice. The subsequent chapters treat classes of tools according to their uses: Digging, raking, and weeding; caring for your lawn; pruning; cutting and splitting wood; watering; and pest control. There is also a chapter on power tool maintenance. Each of these chapters gives you information on how to select, use, and maintain your garden equipment.

So read for awhile. Then enjoy gardening, knowing that your tools are getting the best of care.

New axe

New tools are mass-produced, but they also have special features, like these spring steel fingers which make wood-splitting easier.

Shopping for Garden Equipment

When you shop for garden equipment, keep two rules in mind: (1) always buy the best you can afford and (2) don't buy what you don't need.

Always buy the best you can afford. Before you do anything else, determine the tool's quality. A truly excellent tool is made by skilled craftspeople out of superior materials. This usually means it is expensive. Initially it may hurt to pay top dollar for a tool when you could buy others more cheaply, but it will hurt even more when the cheap tool breaks and you have to buy another one. You can avoid this problem by learning how to evaluate materials and workmanship so that you get the best value for your money.

Don't buy what you don't need. A 20 by 20-foot garden doesn't need a large rotary tiller. And even if you do need a tool that's large or that has a special function, you may need it only once or twice a year. If so, your best bet is to rent it, particularly when dealing with large and expensive machinery (e.g., rotary tillers, ditchdiggers, or powered tree-spraying equipment). The rental cost is only a fraction of the purchase price; in addition, you don't have to maintain, repair, or store that piece of equipment while it sits idle for 364 days out of the year. If you visit several rental agencies in your area and browse through their selection *before* you need something urgently, you will save time later by already knowing what you want.

Before setting off with cash in hand, try to determine, as clearly as possible, what your needs are. Find the chapter that corresponds to the purpose for which you will need tools or equipment, and read it through. See whether you already have a tool that could do the job. If you don't, look for the names and general descriptions of the tools you need. Match the tool to the size of the job. Consider storage space and whether you have room to store the tool properly.

Next, consult garden supply catalogs to survey quality and price ranges.

Consult Local Experts

This book has guidelines for determining the quality of each tool mentioned. Read them before you start shopping. Then, early in your shopping survey, stop in at a rental store and a saw-sharpening shop to talk about tool quality. Rental-equipment owners have a good sense of what equipment they do or don't like and why. Rental tools and equipment must be strong enough to withstand the beating they have to take; otherwise the owners

Before you go to the garden center, be prepared. Shopping guidelines on this page and under each tool throughout the book will save you time and money.

would constantly have to repair or replace the equipment.

The other tradespeople who know tools well are the owners of saw-sharpening shops. These people don't sharpen just saws; they handle anything that might need sharpening, from chainsaws to pruning shears. This makes them more familiar than the average person with the quality of steel and workmanship in a wide variety of tools.

Where to Buy Garden Equipment

When you are ready to buy, make a survey of tool prices and quality among several different hardware or garden equipment stores. Since most of these stores probably carry only two or three brands of garden equipment each, visit several stores to get a wide selection. Ask a salesperson to describe the advantages of the brands carried by that store. After several such talks, you will begin to have a clear idea of the variety of tools available, the prices, and the quality.

What to Look for in Tools

What is quality workmanship? One way to answer this question is in terms of what it *isn't.* Watch out for anything that looks sloppily made, such as screws or bolts that seem to have been placed hurriedly or that are crooked. If the tool has moving parts, work them to see that the action is smooth. Check for burrs or other irregularities on cutting edges.

Does the tool feel comfortable to hold? It

should fit your hand; if it is spring-activated, it shouldn't require more strength than you actually have. Handle the shovels, hoes, and other tools. They should make you *feel* like working: A too-heavy tool won't make you want to use it; a too-light tool may not hold up under strenuous use.

Most manufacturers offer both high-quality and low-quality tools. Many produce "promo" (promotional) tools—a line of tools that is intended to be sold for about half the price of their other tools. For long-term use, these are not worth purchasing.

One guideline is the weight of the tool. Since a heavier weight usually comes from heavier, better-quality material, a heavier shovel generally means that the blade is made of a higher-quality metal than the lightweight ones. This is true of power equipment, as well. Look for heavy metal frames and cowling. In some cases, however, don't overlook plastics—no longer are they necessarily inferior materials. Those tools for which plastics are perfectly acceptable, and even superior to metals, are noted throughout the book.

Power Equipment

When you shop for power equipment, you'll find that electrical tools are generally less expensive and quieter than their gasoline-powered counterparts. However, they have a major limitation: They must be plugged into a power source. But for tools that will always be used within reach of an electrical outlet, you may well prefer the electrical equipment. An electrical motor is apt to be more efficient, more trouble-free, and easier to take care of than a gasoline engine. However, there is some power loss as the electricity runs through the cord, particularly if you have a 50- or 100-foot cord. Lightweight cords lose more electricity and heavyweight cords lose less. The heavier the gauge of the wire in an electrical cord, the longer it can be without losing too much power. You'll need to determine how much power loss is acceptable and determine the length of cord accordingly (see page 78). But before you buy any power equipment, you may want to rent both gas and electrical versions of the same tool to decide which one is more suited to your needs. (For more information on power equipment, see Chapter Six, starting on page 77.)

Once you know the quality and price ranges of the tools or equipment you need, you can shop at two surprisingly excellent sources of these materials—flea markets and garage sales. Tools made 20 or more years ago were often made with more care than they are today. If the tool you want looks slightly damaged, don't immediately cast it aside. Inspect it carefully—a little sharpening or cleaning might make it as good as new. Prices will be lower than for new tools, and the quality may even be better. However, make sure that any used power equipment you buy has a three-prong plug. The third prong—a grounding wire—is an important safety feature.

Using Tools Properly

Tools are made to be strong enough to accomplish the job for which they were designed. If you use a shovel designed for digging and lifting to pry out a stump, you'll probably break the handle. The reason why most tools break is because they are used improperly. This is not to say that you can never use a particular tool for anything other than a narrowly defined purpose. You can certainly use a shovel to separate perennials (even though it won't do the job nearly as well as a nice sharp spade). In fact, gardeners tend to be quite innovative; they use all sorts of things—mixing spoons, old kitchen knives, shingles, and so forth—for weeding or digging. The point is to be aware of your tools' limits and to use the tools only within those limits.

Safety is an extremely important reason for using power tools properly. For example, you may be able to cut brush with a chainsaw, but you run a big risk of having the saw buck and jerk out of control. And an out-of-control chainsaw is a very dangerous piece of equipment. For additional information on safety and safety equipment, see page 95.

Maintaining Hand Tools

If you want your tools to be in good repair, you'll need to develop good maintenance habits. These, like all other habits, are formed by repetition. Follow the tips and techniques described and illustrated in this book; before long, taking good care of your gardening equipment will be automatic. (For detailed information on maintaining engines and power equipment, see Chapter Six, page 77.)

Remember: Cleaning and lubricating your tools makes them last longer and work better; sharpening your tools makes your work easier; and storing your tools in one specific area lets you find them whenever you need them.

Cleaning

If you make a ritual of cleaning your tools after each use, they will reward you by functioning properly. The quickest and easiest way to do this ritual is to hose down all your tools on the way back to the garage or storage shed. If the tool is caked with soil, use a stick or a stiff brush to scrape the soil off. When the tool has no more soil or vegetation, spray the metal part of the tool with a penetrating oil—this kind of oil passes through the water and coats the metal with a thin film. Then hang up your tools to dry. The film of oil will stay on to prevent rust.

Some gardeners clean digging tools by moving them back and forth in a box or 5-gallon bucket filled with a mixture of sand and oil. This process removes light coatings of soil and keeps the tool oiled (if you remember to replenish the oil periodically). Oily particles of sand will stick to the

shovel, but they won't cause any rust and will come right off the next time you dig.

Sharpening

A dull tool is always inefficient. Where a sharp axe bites into wood cleanly, a dull one can ricochet off the wood and cause a serious injury. A dull lawn mower crushes the blades of grass, causing the tops to quickly wither and turn brown. A dull hoe bounces off hard ground rather than sinking into it. Keeping your tools sharpened and using them carefully will make your work much easier and get the job done better and more cleanly.

What makes a tool sharp? When its cutting side is beveled to form a keen edge, it is sharp. The lower the angle of the bevel (that is, the narrower it is), the sharper the tool will be. But the edge of an extremely sharp tool is more likely to get nicked and bent, since it has less metal behind the bevel. Thus, the degree of sharpness desired depends on what use the tool will be put to. Since tools are manufactured with the ideal bevel angle already ground on the basis of intended use, the first rule in sharpening is to follow the existing bevel. The second rule is to remove as little metal as possible; this makes the tool last longer. Sharpening wears down most tools much more than does normal use. So to make your tools last as long as possible, remove as little metal as you can each time you sharpen them.

To keep all your tools sharp, you need the following equipment: A vise, a bench grinder, an electrical drill, a few different types of files, and two or three different types of whetstones.

Sharpening with the Bevel

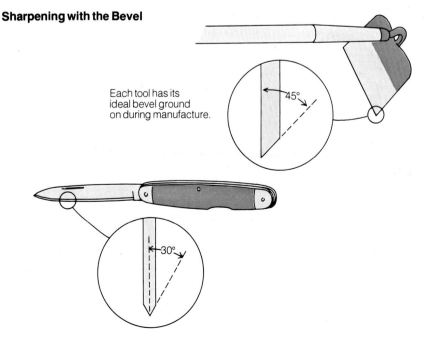

Each tool has its ideal bevel ground on during manufacture.

45°

30°

Bench Grinders are electrical motors that turn abrasive wheels. Many have an abrasive wheel mounted on one side of the motor and a wire brush mounted on the other. The wheel sharpens and the brush removes rust. The grinder sharpens faster but less precisely than hand-held files or whetstones. It also removes metal the fastest and thus produces the most wear. Therefore, be selective when choosing tools to be sharpened by this method. The grinder can quickly shape up badly nicked or dulled tools, such as axes, mattocks, and rotary mower blades. Thereafter, keep them sharp via regular touch-ups with a file or whetstone. When you use a bench grinder, always wear goggles to protect your eyes from flying particles.

Sanders: If you have an electric drill with a grinding disc on it, you can also use it to quickly shape and sharpen a tool. Many hardware stores sell coarse grinding discs for drills, specifically for sharpening tools. These discs, impregnated with a 24-grit aluminum oxide, will sharpen nicked or dull tools, such as hoes, axes, and mattocks.

Files remove metal much more quickly than do whetstones. This makes them best on such tools as spades or hoes but not on finer tools such as jackknives or pruning shears. The cutting edges or serrations on files come in two basic patterns: (1) single cut, known as a mill file, with parallel serrations and (2) double cut, with two serrations that run at opposite angles to form a checkerboard pattern. Single-cut, or mill, files are the best for garden tools. Double-cut files are coarse, remove metal quickly, and remove burrs from the metal. Mill files remove less metal. Therefore, they do a much better job of sharpening.

Since files are designed to be pushed, not pulled, be sure to release all pressure on the backward stroke. Also, never use a file without a handle. The tang (the pointed end of the file) is designed to fit into a wooden handle. Serious injury could result from using the file minus the handle.

Files are graded according to their coarseness. *Coarse* is the roughest grade, followed by *bastard*, *second*, and *smooth* grades. The coarseness also has to do with the length of the file. A 14-inch

Types of Files

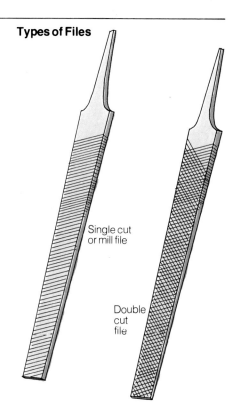

Single cut
or mill file

Double
cut
file

Bench Grinder

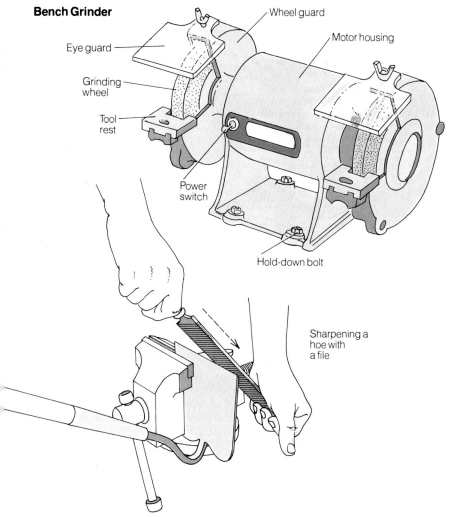

Eye guard

Wheel guard

Motor housing

Grinding
wheel

Tool
rest

Power
switch

Hold-down bolt

Sharpening a
hoe with
a file

File Coarseness

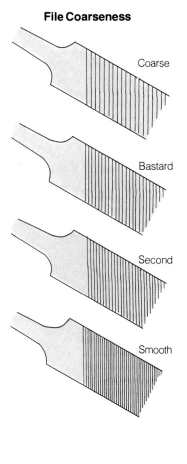

Coarse

Bastard

Second

Smooth

bastard file is coarser than an 8-inch bastard file because its serrations are more widely spaced.

Since files are inexpensive, you may want one of each grade in several different types and lengths. However, a flat 8- to 10-inch bastard file and a flat 8- to 10-inch second file will handle most of your work.

For sharpening saws, however, the files must be fit to the size of the saw's teeth. For sharpening pruning saws, you need a knife file. For sharpening chainsaws, you need a round file. Because saw teeth vary so widely in size and number per inch, it's hard to determine which file best suits your saw. The best method is to take your saw to a saw-sharpening shop or a good hardware store and ask someone there to help you select the proper file.

Files themselves should not be sharpened. However, they do need to be kept clean by periodic scrubbing with a wire brush to remove metal particles between the serrations.

Whetstones are used to hone fine edges or metal that is too hard for the file, particularly on knives, shears, scythes, and axes. Whetstones come in two categories: (1) those that are oiled (oilstones) and (2) those that are not (drystones).

Whetstones usually come in any of three shapes: flat, round, or long and tapered. Each has a specific use.

The drystone has a surface that crumbles away as you use it; thus it constantly renews itself, but also wears out much faster than the oilstone. Generally, the drystone is carried around for on-the-spot sharpening of tools like jackknives.

The oilstone, which is used more commonly, must be kept oiled while in use. Otherwise the metal particles that accumulate from the grinding of the tool will clog the stone's surface, covering it with a glaze that keeps the stone from cutting. When the stone is properly oiled, however, the film of oil floats away the metal particles, thus preventing the stone from clogging.

When you buy a new oilstone, put it in a shallow pan of lightweight, household oil for a day or so and let it soak up as much oil as it can. This treatment will ensure that when a few drops of oil are placed on the surface, they will stay there rather than soaking into the stone right away. Before each use, put a few drops of oil on the stone. After each use, wipe the oil off. Be-

cause the stone is oily, it gathers dust easily, so keep it in a covered case in your workshop.

The flat whetstone (often called a bench stone because it is kept handy on the work bench) is the first choice for general use. It is usually an oilstone. Most often it has a coarse side for sharpening an edge quickly and a smooth side for fine honing. Normally, the stone is kept stationary, and the item to be sharpened is passed back and forth over it.

The round whetstone, which also has coarse and smooth sides, is held in the hand and passed over the item to be sharpened. Its most common use is for sharpening axes and hatchets.

The long, tapered abrasive sticks or rods, which come in a variety of sizes, can be used to sharpen sickles, scythes, scissors, and shears. These sticks or rods generally are drystones.

Lubricating

The only hand tools that require lubrication are those few that have moving parts—for example, pruning tools. Applying a few drops of oil to the moving parts each time you sharpen the tool generally will keep the tool in good working order. Also lubricate the tool if the parts stick or lack their original smooth action. For more information on lubricating and oil, see pages 77 and 89.

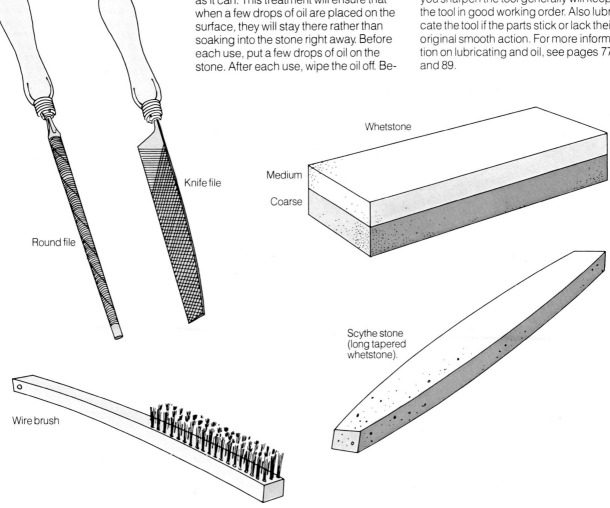

Round file

Knife file

Wire brush

Whetstone

Medium

Coarse

Scythe stone (long tapered whetstone).

Repairs—and How to Avoid Them

When a tool is not used properly and maintained regularly, a variety of problems soon set in: Rust; nicked and dulled cutting edges; and weathered, cracked, or broken handles. Soon you begin to dislike the tool; then you begin to dislike yourself for not fixing it. Here's your chance to shed the guilt complex: Learn to repair and recondition your tools, and renew your resolve to use and care for them properly. This will do wonders for your self-respect (and also for your tools).

Removing and Controlling Rust

Rust, a corrosive process that occurs in iron, is triggered by the presence of water. Therefore, if you keep tools dry and protected from moisture, even from humidity in the air, you won't have rust problems. To prevent rust, keep a protective coat of oil on your tools at all times. While some rust is common on many garden tools and disappears with use, the major rust problems occur when tools are left to lie around outdoors. If you have committed this garden-tool sin, you can resolve to sin no more—but you still need to remedy the current situation.

To remove rust from small tools, such as trowels and pruners, use steel wool or sandpaper.

To remove rust from larger tools, such as shovels and picks, use a wire brush wheel on the end of a power drill. Put the tool in a vise and then clean it until you see only bright metal. If you don't have a power drill, use a wire hand-brush, then scrub well with coarse sandpaper.

If rust is severe, coat the tool with a liquid rust remover (available at most hardware stores). Let it soak in overnight. The next day wipe it off, then use a wire brush and sandpaper to remove all traces of rust.

When the tool is clean, wipe it down with an oily rag, or spray with penetrating oil (see page 7).

Sharpening Nicked or Dulled Cutting Edges

A dulled tool will not cut smoothly. When you find yourself working hard to make a tool do what it was designed to do, it's time to stop and sharpen it. Inspect cutting tools regularly for nicked edges; if you find any, sharpen them off. As part of the same periodic inspection, check all nuts and screws to see that they are tight.

People who work at tool-repair centers commonly complain about bent or sprung shears and pruning tools. A tool gets sprung when its user, finding that it won't cut cleanly through the wood, begins to twist it back and forth to force the cut. Avoid this trap—see page 49 to find out how to use shears properly.

Renewing Roughened and Aged Handles

When wood-handled tools are left out in the elements for a long time, they become dry, cracked, and rough. But don't despair—the handle can be resurrected. If it

Removing Rust

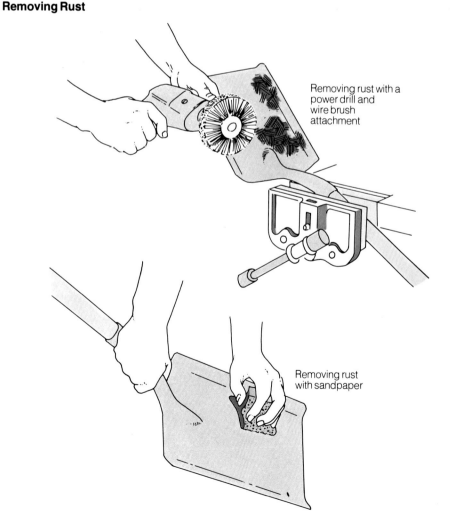

Removing rust with a power drill and wire brush attachment

Removing rust with sandpaper

Smoothing Roughened Handles

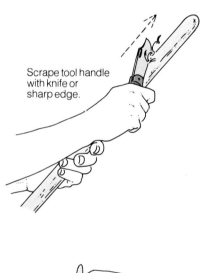

Scrape tool handle with knife or sharp edge.

Paint linseed oil on the smoothed handle.

is rough, scrape it with a knife or sharp edge, file it with a wood rasp, or sand it with coarse or medium sandpaper. Then wipe it down with a damp cloth to remove the fine sawdust from the wood pores. Next, paint the handle with boiled linseed oil. This job is best done during a spell of dry weather (midsummer is ideal) because the drier the wood, the more open the pores; the more open the pores, the better they will absorb the oil. Then place the handle in the sun for a day to let the oil penetrate. For added protection, apply a second coat of linseed oil two days later. Whether you apply one or two coats of oil, the next step is to wipe the handle with a rag that has been soaked in linseed oil. There should be no oil left on the surface, just a very light film. Repeat this process once a year.

Since the handles on new tools come with a light, protective coating of varnish that quickly becomes brittle, you might want to sand off this coating immediately and apply boiled linseed oil.

Repairing Cracked Handles

Handles on shovels, mattocks, and axes receive considerable strain in the course of general use, and sometimes they crack. For a very small crack (less than one-fourth the handle's diameter), wrap the handle twice with black plastic electrician's tape. Carry the wrapping 6 inches beyond each end of the crack. This will help stop the crack from widening. However, it won't restore the handle's original strength, so be careful not to put any undue strain on it after that.

If the crack is any deeper than one-fourth the handle's diameter, rivet the handle as shown on this page, or replace it entirely. It is dangerous to tape deep cracks—the tape might not hold. For instructions on replacing handles, see page 20.

Repairing Cracked Handles

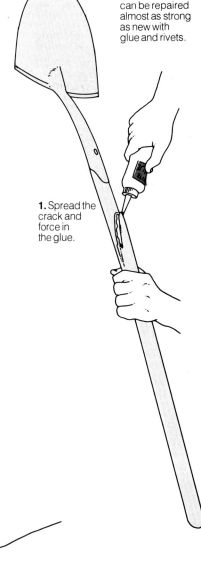

Cracked handles can be repaired almost as strong as new with glue and rivets.

1. Spread the crack and force in the glue.

2. Drill a hole (or two for a long crack) to fit a rivet.

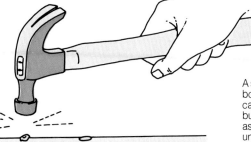

3. Insert a rivet in each hole. Spread the rivet shank and shape it into a flattened dome with a hammer.

A small nut and bolt with washer can also be used, but won't be quite as nice a repair unless countersunk.

Storing Tools and Equipment

The most important part of storing tools is to get them indoors out of the sun, rain, and snow. This will protect them from rust, cracked handles, and all the other problems that come with carelessness. The next most important aspect is to organize your tools. But to many gardeners, "storing" tools means throwing dirty rakes and shovels in a corner of the garage and dropping hand tools on a workbench or in some drawer.

If you've ever stepped on a steel rake and brained yourself with the handle, or if you've ever been unable to find the pruning shears that were there just a minute ago, you've probably promised yourself to reform and organize your tools soon.

The only way to store tools so that you don't trip over them and can find them readily is to hang them on the wall. Then outline each one in paint, or print the name of the tool in the space where it will hang. When you look at the empty but designated space, a sense of order—or of guilt—will propel you to find that tool and put it where it belongs.

Hanging tools on the wall, where they are highly visible, will also encourage you to clean them before you put them away. It's easy to leave a soil-caked shovel in a dark corner, but it's another thing to have to look at it hanging on the wall.

Where to Store Tools

If you are serious about proper storage, the first thing to do is find some storage space.

The garage and basement are logical choices. There must be some wall space somewhere in there—and if not, then it's probably time to clean them and make some room.

But if your garage or basement is a long way from the garden, come up with another place to store your tools; when the storage area is not convenient to the work site, you're more likely to just pile your tools in the nearest corner.

If you have yard space, you might set up a small metal storage building. These buildings, which usually resemble miniature barns, come in prefabricated sections that can be assembled in a single afternoon. However, they usually need some sort of foundation. The best is a poured-concrete slab, but you can also use a wood foundation—old railroad ties, redwood, or preservative-treated wood. Make the interior floor from crushed rock or small gravel, or from bricks laid on a bed of sand. (See Ortho's book, *How to Design and Build Decks and Patios*, for details on making such floors.)

If you want something simpler or less space-consuming, you can put the tools on the outside of the garage wall or on the back of the house near the garden. However, you will need to build a small storage center and attach it to the wall. If the eaves of the house overhang by at least 18 inches, you can build a sort of closet right under the overhang, complete with shelves for storage and doors to protect the tools from the weather. (For details on how to build a storage center, see Ortho's book, *Wood Projects for the Garden*.)

How to Hang Tools

Hanging your garden tools benefits you in several ways: It keeps them out from underfoot; it makes them easy to find; and it keeps them off damp floors that invite rust.

The easiest way to hang tools is simply to drive some nails into the garage or basement wall and hang the tools on the nails. Use 6-penny or 8-penny common nails for shovels and rakes. Put two nails in slightly farther apart than the handle is wide, then hang the tool with the head up.

For smaller hand tools, use 6-penny or 8-penny finishing nails. Because these have no nailhead, you can slip tools with a hole in the handle on or off the nail freely. Or, if you're short on wall space, you can make a multitool hanger, which is essentially the same as the two-nail hanger but instead uses long dowels or 2 by 4s that extend out from the wall. A number of tools can be "stacked" on this rack.

Organize your tools by category. Put all the shovels, spades, and rakes in one area; put all the hand tools, such as clippers and shears, in another area. An additional advantage of labeling or outlining each item's spot on the wall is that you will know when a tool is missing at the end of a day's work.

Storing Garden Tools

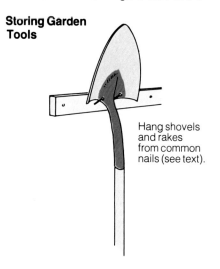

Hang shovels and rakes from common nails (see text).

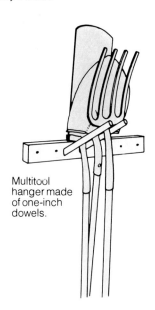

Multitool hanger made of one-inch dowels.

Perfboard Storage Center

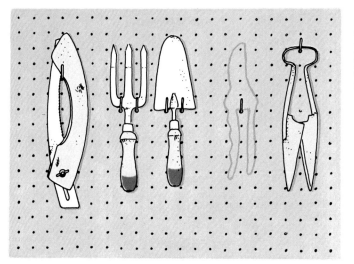

Hang your tools on the wall and outline them, making it obvious when a tool is missing.

Perfboard Storage Center

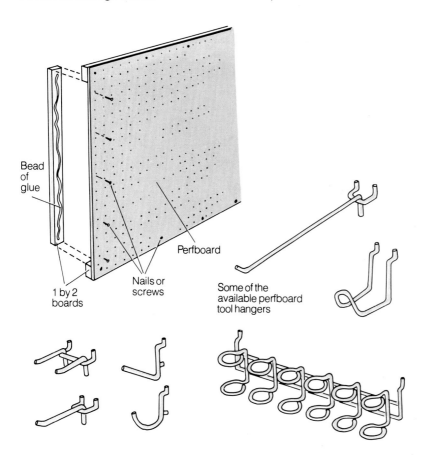

Bead of glue

Perfboard

Nails or screws

1 by 2 boards

Some of the available perfboard tool hangers

Perfboard is a sheet of ⅜-inch-thick hardboard with holes drilled every ½ inch. It is a handy alternative to nails for hanging tools.

Perfboard comes in sheets 4 feet by 8 feet, but it can often be found in smaller sizes in hardware or gardening centers. Since you can cut the sheet to any size you wish, you can make multiple storage centers or use the entire sheet to cover a garage or basement wall.

Since there must be space between the wall and the board in which to fit the hooks, nail and glue a frame made of 1- by 2-inch boards around the back side of the perfboard. Then attach it to the wall.

There is a wide variety of perfboard hooks, made for hanging different types of tools (see the illustrations on this page).

In addition to hooks for small hand tools, most hardware stores carry large S-shape hooks for hanging long-handled tools, such as shovels and rakes.

Storing and Winterizing Hand Tools

Before you put your small hand tools away for the winter, give them just an hour or so of your time. This will probably keep them from rusting and malfunctioning the next spring.

Follow this basic winterizing checklist.

1. Drain the water from all hoses; then coil and hang them so they won't sag and kink. Use hose hangers (available in hardware stores, or make your own from an old automobile wheel fastened to the wall).

2. Clean *all* tools, from sprayers to sprinklers, from shears to shovels. Use a wire brush to remove any caked-on dirt or vegetation. Lubricate all pivot points and springs, then spray all bare metal parts and cutting edges with penetrating oil to prevent rust.

3. Check all hand tools for loose screws or nuts and tighten where necessary. Check for any broken or bent parts and replace or repair them.

4. Wipe all wooden handles down with boiled linseed oil. You can also substitute regular linseed oil, but first warm it to make it penetrate the wood more deeply. Just place the can in a pot of boiling water for two or three minutes.

5. Sharpen all cutting edges, then wipe down the blades with an oily rag or spray with penetrating oil.

6. Hang the tools in their proper storage spot so you can find them next season.

Storing and Winterizing Power Equipment

As with hand tools, you should clean and keep off damp floors all your power equipment, whether lawn mowers, edgers, or chainsaws. If your basement or garage floor gets wet during the winter, raise the equipment onto a small platform made from boards or a sheet of ½-inch plywood laid over several lengths of 2- by 4-inch boards.

When you put away your gasoline-powered equipment for the winter, make sure that it will be in good condition for the next season by following these steps.

1. Clean and wipe the equipment. Remove all collected grease, dirt, and vegetation.

2. Check for any loose screws or nuts. Tighten everything down.

3. Sharpen all cutting edges (see pages 7–9) and then wipe all bare metal parts with an oily rag or spray with a penetrating oil.

4. Change the oil if your equipment has a four-cycle engine (see page 89).

5. Clean and oil the air filter.

6. Remove the gasoline from the tank. If the engine is small enough, you can just tip it on its side; otherwise, remove the fuel line. After the tank is drained, remove all gas from the fuel line and carburetor by starting the engine and running it until it stops. If gasoline is left in the tank all winter, it will turn stale and collect water droplets from condensation.

7. Remove and clean the spark plug. Replace it if it is worn. Squirt a little oil into the spark plug hole and then pull the starting rope several times to turn the engine over and distribute the oil around the piston. Replace the plug.

8. Check for any worn or damaged parts. Order the replacements now so that your equipment will be ready to operate when the next season begins.

Platform for Equipment Storage

2 by 4s

½-inch plywood

DIGGING, RAKING, AND WEEDING

Learn when to use a spade instead of a shovel, how to sharpen a hoe, or what type of tiller will work for you. From trowels to rotary tillers, this chapter offers clear descriptions and illustrations of the full range of digging, raking, and weeding tools.

If you are like many gardeners, you have just one shovel that you use for digging up the garden, planting trees, or digging a ditch. A shovel is an invaluable tool, but if you have trouble cutting straight borders with it you might want to invest in a square-nose spade. This tool will make it easier to cut straight edges along borders, remove sod, or transplant trees. Both common and specialized tools have been designed with variations to make specific tasks easier.

Selecting Quality Tools

The quality of steel used in tools for digging, raking, and weeding has much to do with the tool's durability. Although tools are not normally stamped with the type of steel used, the following information will help you spot quality steel as well as other construction features common to tools in this category:

☐ A stainless steel tool is the top of the line and therefore very expensive. Its advantages are indisputable: It is very hard and virtually rust-proof, and soil will not readily stick to it.

☐ Carbon manganese steel is used to make some of the better gardening tools in this country. Others are imported from England, which has a long history of producing high-quality gardening tools. Ask a salesperson to locate some catalogs so that you can read a detailed description of how the tools are made. Read over the comments of several firms, and compare.

☐ Check to see how the handle is at-

Springtime is a gardener's joy. Make planting easier with the right tools.

tached to the working end of the tool. On most shovels, the back of the socket does not fully enclose the handle. This "open socket" construction is of cheaper quality than the "closed socket," which is either seamless or welded closed down the back.

Rakes and hoes usually are attached to a handle by means of the "tang-and-ferrule" system. The head ends in a long protrusion (tang) instead of a socket. This tang is fitted into a hole in the end of the handle. The handle end then is wrapped with a piece of light metal (the ferrule), which is held in place by a pin or rivet.

The tang can become loose, either through use or because the handle cracks or rots near its end. This loosening then causes the head of the tool to loosen. On better tools, the head and socket are made from a single piece of steel, and the handle is fitted into the socket.

☐ Inspect the wooden handle. It should be made from straight-grained ash or hickory, and it should be smooth and free of any knots or blemishes. For maximum strength, the grain in the handle should run in the same direction as the direction of the force or pressure that's exerted on the tool during use. The handle should fit tightly and evenly into the socket or ferrule. If the head wiggles or if any of the workmanship looks careless, the tool will not last, even under normal use.

Try Before You Buy

Tools such as shovels, rakes, picks, and hoes vary in terms of weight and balance. If you already have one or more of these tools, you probably already know each one's particular weight and balance and feel quite comfortable with it. A different tool might feel strange and uncomfortable

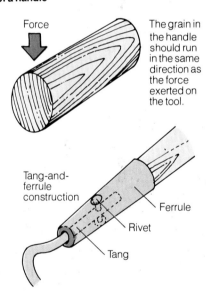

Cross-section of a handle

Force

The grain in the handle should run in the same direction as the force exerted on the tool.

Tang-and-ferrule construction

Ferrule

Rivet

Tang

in your hands. So if it's time to replace an old, comfortable tool, try to find one of the same make and size as the original.

If you are about to buy a tool for the very first time, start out by renting one or borrowing a neighbor's. Neighbors are sure to be delighted to let you dig and chop weeds in their garden, while they stand by and describe the joy of owning such a tool. Try several different sizes and lengths until you find one that feels right to you; then buy one like it.

A certain tool may come in many different sizes and lengths. Evaluate each tool's features in terms of your own needs before you buy. And be realistic about your strength: A tool that is too heavy will make gardening a burdensome chore rather than the pleasure it might otherwise be.

TROWELS

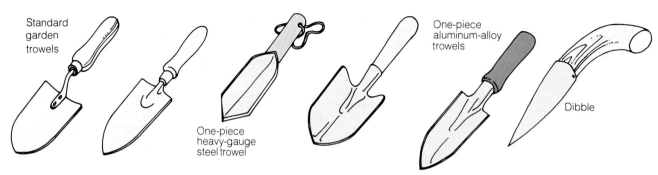

Standard garden trowels

One-piece heavy-gauge steel trowel

One-piece aluminum-alloy trowels

Dibble

Trowels tend to be very attractive, and it's hard to know which one is best until you have tried several. Trowel blades differ in width, length, and amount of cup in the blade. The narrow, sharp blade is good for digging out stubborn weeds in the lawn; the broader, flatter blades are good for general garden work, as they move more soil and make larger holes.

Cup of Blade

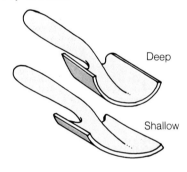

Deep

Shallow

The most common problem, especially on cheap models, is that the tine may bend. (On a trowel, the tine connects the blade to the handle.) The best solution is to buy a top-quality trowel made from a single piece of metal. Aluminum alloy or plated steel are among the strongest, and they resist rusting.

Handles can be made of wood, metal, or plastic. Try several to find one that feels right to you. A larger handle tends to be more comfortable—you don't have to close your hand as tightly to grip it. A bright-colored handle is easier to spot when mislaid in the garden. If you buy a top-quality trowel, get one with a colorful handle, and keep close tabs on it. Some gardeners have given up keeping track of these and have opted to buy several cheaper ones, instead.

Types of Trowels

One-Piece Aluminum-Alloy Trowel

The one-piece aluminum-alloy trowel is an excellent choice for general gardening work. The handle is slightly curved to fit your palm comfortably. With some, the handle is encased in bright-colored plastic, making it highly visible. These trowels come in a variety of blade shapes and sizes. You might want a narrow, sharp type as well as the broader type.

Standard Garden Trowel

The blade of the standard garden trowel fits into the handle via the tang-and-ferrule system. Ask the salesperson to help you select the best quality; this style tends to bend and work loose from the handle. Select one with high-quality steel that is chrome plated to resist rusting. Eventually the chrome plating will wear off, so it's especially important to store it clean and oiled to prevent rust.

One-Piece Heavy-Gauge Steel Trowel

The one-piece heavy-gauge steel trowel is one of the strongest models on the market. The 3-inch-wide blade is V-shaped rather than cupped, which makes it almost impossible to bend. It can be used for digging out rocks or furrowing. To quickly transplant seedlings (e.g., tomatoes and peppers), hold the trowel with the blade pointed straight down, jam it into the earth, and wiggle it back and forth a few times. Remove it, set the seedling in the hole, and pack the dirt around it.

Dibble

The dibble, sometimes called a dibber, is a pointed tool that's used to make holes in the ground for transplanting seedlings, flowers, or bulbs. The 4- to 5-inch-long, round, tapered blade is about 2 inches in diameter at the top and pointed on the end. You can easily make your own dibble by sharpening a short length of branch or scrap 2 by 2 or by buying a hardwood tentpeg in a sporting goods shop.

Maintenance

Stainless-steel, all-plastic, and aluminum-alloy trowels are virtually indestructible and need almost no maintenance. However, a standard garden trowel with tang-and-ferrule construction should be cleaned carefully.

Transplanting with a Trowel

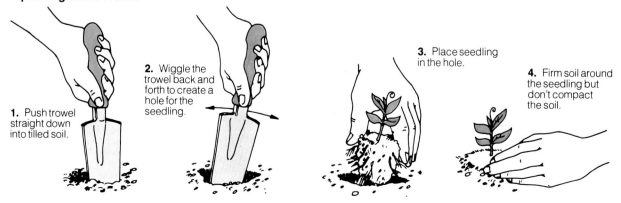

1. Push trowel straight down into tilled soil.

2. Wiggle the trowel back and forth to create a hole for the seedling.

3. Place seedling in the hole.

4. Firm soil around the seedling but don't compact the soil.

SHOVELS, SPADES, AND FORKS

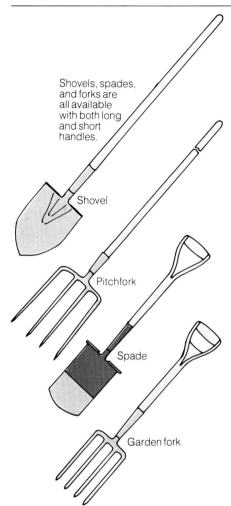

Shovels, spades, and forks are all available with both long and short handles.

Shovel

Pitchfork

Spade

Garden fork

How do you know whether to buy a shovel, a spade, a fork, or all three? The decision depends primarily on two factors: (1) what kind of garden soil you have (a heavy-clay soil is difficult to work; very sandy or light soil is easy to work) and (2) what kind of gardening you do (digging trenches, turning over garden soil, scooping up sawdust, or all of these).

Shovels. Shovels can be used for both digging and lifting, although they are primarily designed for lifting loose soil or other materials. If you're moving lightweight materials such as sawdust, a wide-scoop shovel is best; if you're working with concrete, use a strong square-nose shovel. A general-purpose round-point garden shovel is good for digging in average garden soil, and is the best type to buy.

If you like to dig in the garden for exercise and enjoyment but don't consider yourself particularly strong, select a small, pointed shovel or narrow spade. That way you won't have to lift so much soil each time—and when you get tired of digging, you may find that the smaller shovel just fits child-size hands, as well.

Spades. Cutting and digging in heavy soil is best accomplished with a spade. The spade is designed not only to cut soil but also (because of its square nose and flat blade) to dig straight-sided, flat-bottomed trenches and to remove a layer of sod.

Forks. There are basically two types of forks: (1) garden forks and (2) pitchforks. Garden forks have thick, heavy tines and are used to turn over soil. Pitchforks have lighter, longer tines and are used to move light, loose material. A garden fork works best in gravelly soil or in very good garden soil (soil with lots of organic matter). It penetrates the soil and breaks up clods better than a shovel or spade.

Handles

Handles on shovels, spades, and forks come in two types: (1) long and straight and (2) short, with a D-shape grip. When you use tools with long, straight handles, you can dig deeper holes without having to do much bending, and you can throw soil farther, when necessary. Shorter, D-shape tools give you more control and are good for delicate work (e.g., working around tree roots or dividing perennial plants). They are also good for digging trenches and for working in close quarters (e.g., in a greenhouse or against the side of a house or tree where your digging is crowded). In addition, they fit well in the trunk of your car for camping trips.

The wood on handles normally comes from ash or hickory, both of which are strong and lightweight. The handles on

cheaper tools may be made from Douglas fir, which is not as strong or resilient. Before you buy, have the salesperson check the catalogs and confirm the type of wood used. A few shovels have handles of rolled (tubular) steel, but these are heavy, expensive, and designed primarily for use in nurseries.

On shovels and pitchforks, the length of the handles generally ranges from 40 to 48 inches. The handles are slightly tapered, for comfort in handling. Spades and garden forks commonly have D-handles, which range in length from 26 to 30 inches. Some D-handles are made of wood that is wrapped in metal; some are all wood; and some (the cheapest) have a light metal alloy handle attached to the wood. However, this will not hold up under extensive use.

The best handles are manufactured in this way: First the wood is split at the top; then it is steamed to become flexible; and, finally, it is placed in molds to be shaped. Then the wood grip is glued and riveted to the frame. Some heavy-duty models are further reinforced with a wood filler in the Y of the handle.

One variation on the D-handle is the T-head. This style is good for large or small hands that don't fit comfortably around a D-handle.

Construction

Shovels and Spades. There are two basic ways of constructing shovels and spades: (1) the "open back" and (2) the

Handles

D-handle

Reinforced D-handle

T-handle

Shovel Construction

Open Back

Rivets

Crimp (frog)

Closed Back

Rivets through side

Closed back metal triangle is welded over crimp (frog) for greater strength.

Lock Socket

Rivets through to top

Front strap and blade are one piece with preformed back strap welded into place.

Forged Socket and Shank

"closed back." The open back is the cheapest and most common. The blade is stamped out of a single sheet of metal, and the back of the socket is left open to be fitted around the handle. This method of construction requires a crimp ("frog") on the face of the blade below the socket to provide additional rigidity. The back of the blade is correspondingly hollow at this point.

The closed back is more expensive and sturdier. It is forged rather than stamped. Its seamless socket fully encloses a carefully fitted handle. The blade is so strong that no reinforcing "frog" is required. This type of shovel or spade is often made out of high-carbon steel or steel and manganese for greater strength. The gauge is a measure of the thickness of the metal. The smaller the number, the thicker and more expensive the tool. Although the forged-steel spade is more expensive, if given proper care it can be handed down to your grandchildren.

Because spades are used to pry and lift heavy sod, soil, or rocks, they have a heavier construction than most shovels. When you buy a spade, select one that has a long socket for additional strength.

Forks. As with shovels and spades, in a good-quality fork the tines and socket are forged from a single piece of steel. Cheaper forks use the "tang-and-ferrule" system (see page 15), which will not hold up as long as a socket.

Blades and Tines

Blades. The blades of a shovel can be: (1) pointed, (2) moderately pointed or rounded, or (3) square. The first type is primarily for digging, the last type is exclusively for moving loose materials, and the middle type is a general-purpose shovel used for both digging and lifting.

A general-purpose garden shovel is about 8 to 9 inches wide. The wider the blade, the more material you can move —but the more strength you will need. If you are among those less physically inclined, choose a shovel with 6-inch-wide blades. These are excellent for digging narrow trenches (e.g., for underground sprinkler pipes). With spades, the blade widths vary only slightly. On the best shovels and spades, the blades are always forged, not stamped.

One feature to look for is the angle of the shovel blade in relation to the handle— that is, the degree of cant. Because of its straight line, a shovel with little or no cant is excellent for digging holes but less than ideal for scraping up loose earth (to make the blade lie flat on the ground, you would have to bend over uncomfortably).

A shovel with considerable cant provides more leverage when you're prying up heavy earth. However, it is awkward to dig straight down with a high-cant shovel —you have to hold the handle at some distance from you in order to keep the blade perpendicular to the ground.

Tines. Most garden forks have only four tines, but the heads differ slightly in width and length. The wider and longer the head, the deeper you can dig. But the deeper you dig, the more likely you are to turn up a backbreaking amount of soil at a time. So choose the size of your fork with your own strength in mind.

The tines on garden forks also differ slightly, according to their purpose. For example, a heavy-duty garden fork, sometimes called an English digging fork, has square tines that provide increased strength. Select this superior-quality fork if your soil is rocky or contains much heavy clay.

Whichever fork you choose, make sure it's made of high-quality steel that resists being bent out of position. Pulling a fork back to loosen the soil strains the tines, so the stronger they are, the less they will bend (however, tines *do* bend occasionally). If you use the fork properly and avoid unnecessary prying, you should have few problems.

Types of Shovels

Pointed and Medium-Point Shovels
These general-purpose, medium-weight (3¼- to 4½-pound) shovels are the first choice of many gardeners. They have long, straight handles and flat or rolled footrests. Both the sharp and the medium points are good for cutting through hard soil or roots. If the shovel has a moderate cant, it can be used equally well to dig soil or to move it.

Round-Nose Shovel
This shovel is somewhat broader than the common round-point shovel, which makes it excellent for moving loose soil or sand.

Types of Shovels

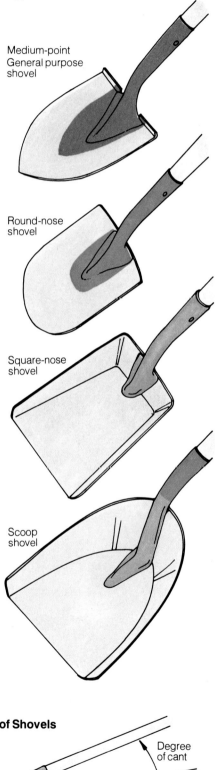

Medium-point General purpose shovel

Round-nose shovel

Square-nose shovel

Scoop shovel

Garden Fork Tines

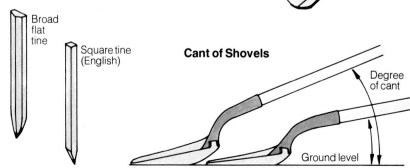

Broad flat tine

Square tine (English)

Cant of Shovels

Degree of cant

Ground level

The blade should have considerable cant in relation to the handle so that you can scoop up soil or other material without having to stoop down excessively. This shovel is popular with gardeners who have irrigation ditches in their gardens—its broad face and rounded nose make it easy to form and clean the ditches.

Narrow-Blade Shovel
The blade on this shovel (about 9 inches long and from 4 to 6 inches wide) is about half the size of the blade on a standard shovel. A specialty shovel (sometimes called a trenching shovel), it is used primarily for working in narrow border-gardens or for digging narrow ditches (e.g., for underground sprinkler pipes). Its small size makes it convenient for the elderly or the very young to use. And if you happen to live near the coast, you can use it for digging clams.

Square-Nose Shovel
The square-nose shovel has a square end, a flat (rather than rounded) face, and sides that angle upward to hold material in. It is excellent for moving large amounts of loose material (e.g., earth, sand, gravel, or sawdust) or for mixing materials on a hard surface. Because it is used primarily for scooping, it has a fairly high blade-to-handle cant to reduce the amount of stooping required. This type of shovel is available with either the long, straight handle or the shorter D-handle.

The square-nose shovel is often used by people who do occasional work with concrete, since its flat bottom and square nose make it convenient for mixing concrete, whether in a wheelbarrow or on the ground.

Scoop Shovel
The scoop shovel tends to be twice the size of a square-nose shovel. It is designed to let you quickly handle large amounts of light material (e.g., grain, sawdust, or snow). Other shovels are made from steel, but the scoop shovel is usually made from an aluminum alloy, which makes it light. Therefore, it is not strong enough to use for tough digging or moving chores. It can, however, be used to move sacks or heavy rocks; just skid the loaded shovel along the ground.

Types of Spades

Medium Garden Spade
The medium garden spade is the all-around spade for the average gardener. The blade is about 8 inches wide and 12 inches long, and the socket on a quality spade is about 10 inches long. It has a flat or rolled footrest and a low blade-to-handle cant, which enables you to work with-

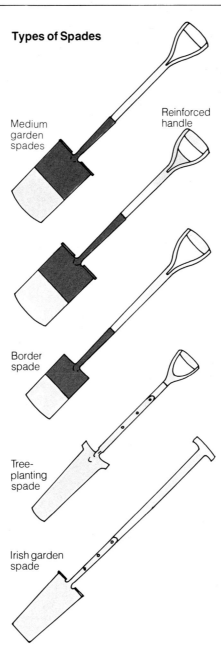

Types of Spades

Medium garden spades

Reinforced handle

Border spade

Tree-planting spade

Irish garden spade

out bending too much when cutting border edges or digging straight-sided holes for trenches or trees.

Heavy-Duty Garden Spade
The heavy-duty garden spade differs from the medium spade in several significant ways. First, the blade is the same size, but the socket is two or three inches longer. Second, on a quality tool the Y of the handle is filled with a piece of hardwood for greater rigidity. The heavy-duty spade also has a higher degree of cant, which gives the greater power that's required in order to pry up heavy soil or rocks. Only if you do this kind of strenuous work will you need this type of spade.

Border Spade
Because the border spade is smaller all around, it is ideal for more confined areas (e.g., border gardens). Since the head is only about 5 inches by 9 inches, the spade weighs less than 4 pounds. Compare this to about 4½ pounds for a medium spade and more than 6 pounds for a heavy-duty spade.

Tree-Planting Spade
The tree-planting spade is a specialty tool, but it is worthwhile if you are planning to plant or transplant a half-dozen or more trees. A quality tree-planting spade has a wide footrest but a blade that's long and narrow (about 7 by 16 inches). The curved blade makes it easier to dig round holes for planting trees. Because the handle is subjected to great strain when the spade is used for prying and lifting soil from a deep hole, buy a spade with an extra-long socket or with forged-steel straps that extend more than half the handle's length.

Irish Garden Spade
The Irish garden spade is a versatile tool that's used for standard spading, working on borders, or planting trees. The distinctive T-handle adapts to both big and small hands, and its greater length (35 to 40 inches) is useful for digging deep holes or trenches. It is the favorite of gardeners who like to double-dig a garden. Where other spades have a socket, a quality Irish spade has straps that run up a third of the handle. These straps, which are forged as part of the blade, provide more flex and strength than a socket.

Types of Forks

Medium Garden Fork
Medium garden forks have a 7- to 8-inch-wide head and 10- to 12-inch-long tines. The medium width of the tines makes them suitable both for digging heavy soil and for lifting and moving loose earth. The handle should be made of straight-grained ash or hickory and be formed in a D.

Heavy-Duty Garden Fork
Choose a heavy-duty garden fork if your soil is rocky or contains much heavy clay. The fork has an approximately 8- by 12-inch head and weighs nearly 6 pounds (compared to about 4 pounds for a medium fork). It may have square tines for increased strength. The socket is longer than that on medium forks to give the handle additional strength. On a good tang-and-ferrule-style, heavy-duty fork, the steel ferrule also is longer, and for the same reason. The wood or steel D-handle on this fork may also be reinforced across the Y.

Types of Forks

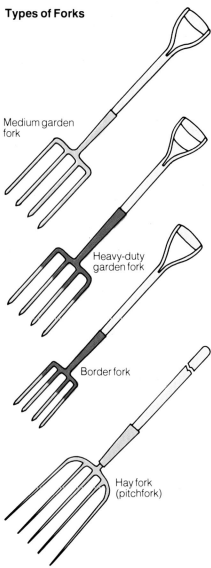

Medium garden fork

Heavy-duty garden fork

Border fork

Hay fork (pitchfork)

great strength and flexibility. Handle lengths range from 4 to 5 feet.

Maintenance

Cleaning
Always clean your digging tools after using them—follow the guidelines outlined on pages 7–9.

Hollow-back (open-back) shovels collect dirt in the hollow and in the base of the socket. Check to make sure these parts are clean. Then oil the shovel lightly and put it away. And remember to take care of the handle, too—sand off the protective varnish before using the shovel for the first time. Then, once a year, give it a good rubdown with boiled linseed oil.

Sharpening
Rarely do shovels need sharpening. Forged shovels, for example, are self-sharpening; stamped shovels are never sharpened. However, keep spades sharp if they are used for cutting (their intended purpose). Use a file to touch up the double

bevel of a spade. Place the spade horizontally in a vise or put it on the ground with the blade pointing away from you. With a bastard mill file, make one continuous motion across the spade edge from one side to the other. Then turn the spade over and repeat the process on the other bevel. Follow the instructions on pages 8–9 for sharpening with files. The objective is to give the spade the same sharpness it had when you first bought it.

Replacing Broken Handles
Using a shovel improperly—for example, as a prybar to move rocks or to break up heavy clay—is the reason why handles get broken. A cracked handle can be repaired (see p. 11) but the best solution is to replace the entire handle. The hardest part is removing the handle from the socket. However, if you follow these steps carefully, you will end up with a tool that's good as new.

Border Fork
A border fork is like a medium garden fork, except that the head is about half the standard size (i.e., about 5 by 9 inches or smaller). This fork also has four tines, but here they are broader so that they can hold more soil. The handles remain the same length as for standard garden forks (about 28 inches). These smaller forks are used for working in border gardens, as the name implies, but they are also good general-pupose tools for younger or older persons with less strength. The tool weighs about 3 pounds.

Hay Fork (Pitchfork)
A hay fork, or pitchfork, has three or four 12-inch-long tines that are round and tapered to easily slip in and out of hay. Since it is not meant for digging, it has no footrest. The handle on a pitchfork is straight-grained ash or hickory, two woods with

Replacing a Broken Shovel Handle

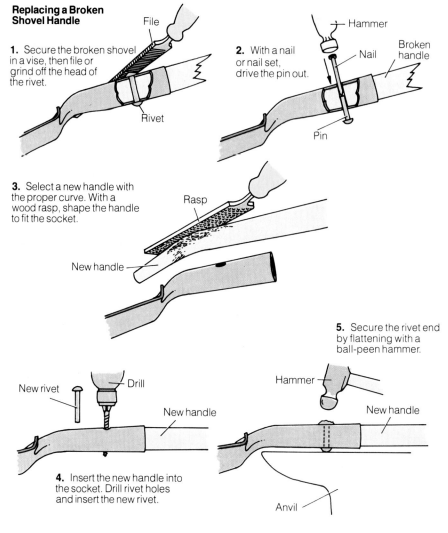

1. Secure the broken shovel in a vise, then file or grind off the head of the rivet.

File

Rivet

2. With a nail or nail set, drive the pin out.

Hammer

Nail

Broken handle

Pin

3. Select a new handle with the proper curve. With a wood rasp, shape the handle to fit the socket.

Rasp

New handle

5. Secure the rivet end by flattening with a ball-peen hammer.

Hammer

New handle

Anvil

New rivet

Drill

New handle

4. Insert the new handle into the socket. Drill rivet holes and insert the new rivet.

PICKS AND MATTOCKS

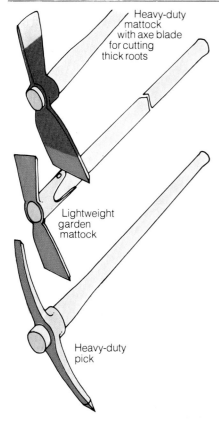

Heavy-duty mattock with axe blade for cutting thick roots

Lightweight garden mattock

Heavy-duty pick

Picks and mattocks are designed to work in ground that is too hard, rocky, or root-filled for a shovel, spade, or fork.

Picks are for loosening soil that is very hard and very rocky. One end is usually pointed to do the initial breaking of hard ground; the other end has a narrow (about 1-inch-wide), chisel-like tip for scraping an area or working somewhat softer ground.

Mattocks are for loosening soil that is hard but not rock-hard, that is laced with roots, or that is full of stumps. Two sizes are available: (1) the lightweight garden mattocks (about 2½ pounds) and (2) the heavy-duty mattock (5 pounds). One side of the mattock blade resembles a small but thick axehead and is used for cutting large roots; the other side has a flat, hoelike head for moving soil and cutting small or medium-size roots. Mattocks are also handy for digging narrow ditches. Because the head is only 4 inches wide and because mattocks have a lot of chopping power, you can dig a ditch as narrow as 6 inches wide and as deep as 1 or 2 feet.

Picks and mattocks vary in terms of the weight of steel used in the head and in the length of the handle. If you are tall and hefty and are working on a big job, choose a tool with a long handle and a heavy head. If either you or the job are smaller, however, get something more in proportion to your needs.

The heads of picks and mattocks are attached to their handles by an eye. The wooden handle is fitted tightly in a hole—the "eye"—in the metal head and held in place by friction. (See "Maintenance," page 22, to find out how this is done.) When you select these tools, be sure that this fitting is secure; during use, check regularly for any loosening.

The styles of picks and mattocks vary primarily on the basis of the weight of the material from which they are made. In addition, other tools that are similar to mattocks are available. To be sure that some of these tools fit your needs and are made of good-quality materials, ask the salespeople to carefully explain the tools' design and purpose.

Using a Pick or Mattock

There are two schools of thought on how to use these tools. One is to put your left hand close to the tool's head and your right hand close to the end of the handle. (If you're left handed, do the reverse.) Stand with your feet planted apart, raise the pick straight up, and push it into the air directly over your head. Let it fall without forcing it, until it reaches its target. Tighten your grip as the tool enters the soil. Then, with a small snap or uplift, pop it loose from the

Using a Mattock

soil. If your rhythm is regular, you can keep up this motion for quite a while, especially if you learn to alternate hands.

The other method is to put your right hand close to the tool's head and your left hand close to the end of the handle. Plant your feet apart and swing the pick back past your legs on your right side and then over your head and down into the ground in one smooth arc. Your right hand will slide back to the end of the handle where your left hand is gripping.

Alternate hands and trade sides with your swing to avoid straining one side of your body.

Whichever method you use, the most important factor is safety. Those who favor the second method say that the centrifugal force prevents the head from slipping down and hitting you. Those who favor the first method say that a properly seated head should not slip at all and that this method limits the danger of missing your target. Caution is advised for both.

Maintenance

Cleaning and Storage

Since mattocks and picks tend to be used only infrequently, storage is particularly important. Be sure to remove all dirt and to wipe the tools with an oily rag before put-

One method for using a pick or mattock is to use a fluid motion in a circular pattern as illustrated. Let the weight of the tool work for you. Alternate sides after 3 or 4 times to balance muscle stress.

Another method is to raise the pick or mattock directly overhead, then thrust it down—using its own weight to finish the stroke.

ting them away. If the handle gets wet, knock the head loose and remove it so that the handle can dry. To do this, hold onto the head with both hands, and pound the other end of the handle on a hard surface. This will knock the handle loose so that you can pull it through the eye of the mattock. If the tool is stored wet, the head of the handle can develop dry rot inside.

Sharpening

It's possible to go for years without having to put a new edge on a pick. However, when it *is* time to touch up the ends, place the head in a vise and sand it with a belt sander fitted with an abrasive belt—or do it the hard way, using a 14-inch coarse file. Leave at least ⅛ inch of metal near the edge so it will not chip or bend.

Mattocks are sharpened like picks—instead of making the blade very sharp, maintain the original bevel angle (in this case, about 45 degrees). A too-sharp edge will become deformed as soon as it hits the first rock.

To sharpen a mattock properly, remove the head and place it in a vise. Start with a coarse file, then switch to a bastard mill file. Then use any of the following: A belt or disc sander with an aluminum oxide abrasive belt, a 40-60 grit Carborundum belt, or a grindstone. Move your sharpening tool back and forth across the blade of the pick, matching the angle at which you hone it to its original bevel angle to prevent any rounding of the bevel or any cupping of the blade.

Replacing Handles

Both picks and mattocks need a handle that fits properly. Wooden handles that become cracked or broken must be replaced with new handles.

New handles for these or any other eyed tools are purposely made oversize; this allows you to fit them by hand and make sure that the friction fit is as tight as need be. For the friction fit to work properly, the wood should touch as much of the metal on the inside of the eye as possible. Most handles don't require any adjustment; however, if yours does, the following steps will ensure a good fit:

1. Using lubricating graphite or a graphite pencil, smear graphite on the inside of the eye.

2. Seat the new handle firmly in the head.

3. Remove the handle.

4. Remove all graphite smudges left from where the wood came into contact with the metal. Use a wood rasp for the removal. Repeat this process until the graphite shows that the wood is in contact with the metal over almost the entire surface of the inside of the eye.

5. At this point the handle probably is still protruding past the head a few inches. Saw it down so that it protrudes only about ½ inch from the head. Then, holding the handle at the other end, drop the mattock on a hard surface (e.g., a sidewalk or driveway) so that the ½-inch protrusion hits the surface. Do this a couple of times. The head will then fit very tightly. However, you will still be able to remove it for storage or sharpening.

Removing the Head of a Pick or Mattock

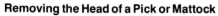

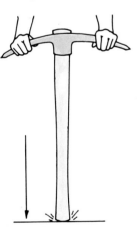

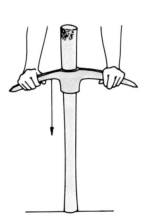

Grasp the head firmly and knock the handle against a hard surface.

When the handle becomes loose, remove the head from the handle.

Replacing the Handle on a Pick or Mattock

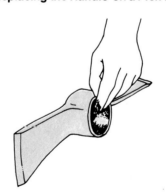

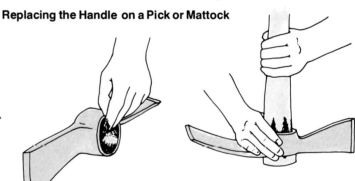

1. Use lubricating graphite and smear it on the inside of the eye.

2. Seat the new handle firmly in the head. The graphite will mark the contact points between wood and metal.

Sharpening a Mattock

Remove the head and place securely in a vise. Use a belt sander with a 40–60 grit belt or a grindstone to regain the original bevel. Finish with a file.

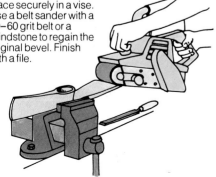

3 and 4. Remove the handle. Using a wood rasp, file all areas where the metal and wood made contact, indicated by the graphite smudges. Repeat this process until almost the entire eye is in contact with the new handle.

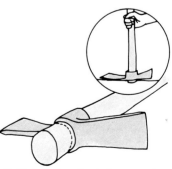

5. Slide the head onto the rasped area. Seat it firmly. Cut handle so that ½ inch remains above head. Seat the head again by dropping it onto a hard surface.

POSTHOLE DIGGERS

Post Hole Diggers

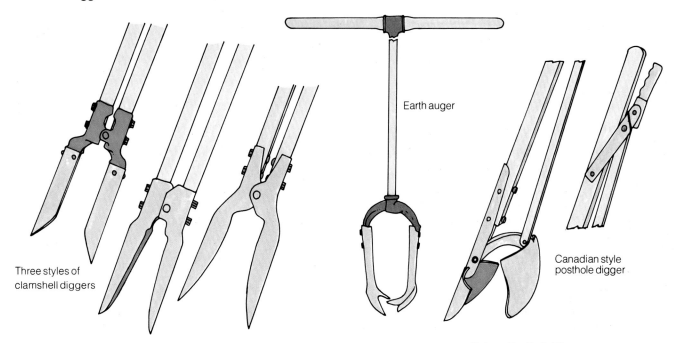

Earth auger

Three styles of clamshell diggers

Canadian style posthole digger

If you have a lot of fences to build and maintain, you can make the job easier by buying or renting a posthole digger.

In selecting a posthole digger, consider these factors: Your type of ground, the depth of hole you'll need, how often you'll use the digger, and the extent of your own strength. If you need holes up to 2 feet deep, the clamshell digger is the best general-purpose tool. Auger-type diggers work for holes of any depth, but because they are less strong than the clamshell, they are less effective in hard, rocky soil. If you will need to dig many holes, think about renting a gasoline-powered auger.

Whichever type you select, look for quality-steel blades and good-quality handles of straight-grained ash or hickory.

Types of Posthole Diggers

Clamshell Digger
Among home gardeners, the clamshell digger is the most common type. It works with a scissor action. The two handles are about 4 feet long, and the blades add another 9 to 12 inches. When you push the handles together, the two curved blades open. Jam the digger into the soil; then pull the handles apart. This closes the blades around the earth so that you can lift it out.

Earth Auger
Another type of posthole digger—essentially an earth auger—has two stationary blades on the end of a steel rod. The tips of the blades are bent inward at right angles

and slightly offset from each other. The rod is twisted by the handle on top and the blades screw themselves into the ground. When they are filled with earth, lift out the digger, remove the soil, and repeat the process. This type of digger is fine for soft soil only, not for hard or rocky soil.

Canadian Model
There is a posthole digger made in Canada that combines a fixed blade and a movable blade. The fixed blade digs into the soil; the movable blade, operated by a lever on the handle, closes on the fixed blade to seize the soil.

Maintenance

Cleaning
Before storing any posthole digger, clean and oil its blades (particularly the scissor mechanism on a clamshell digger). This will keep the tool in good working condition.

Sharpening
Extensive use will make the blades of a clamshell digger become dulled, bent, or chipped. When working far from the workshop, it's wise to keep an 8-inch bastard file in your pocket; you can use it to periodically touch up the blade ends. File only the inside of the blades, and keep the bevel at between 60 and 80 degrees—this will keep lots of steel behind the edge to help prevent it from bending or breaking.

Regularly check the bolts and nuts holding the blades to the handle: They should be tight.

Using a Posthole Digger

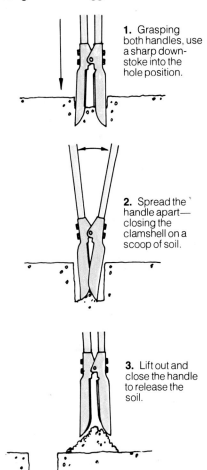

1. Grasping both handles, use a sharp downstoke into the hole position.

2. Spread the handle apart—closing the clamshell on a scoop of soil.

3. Lift out and close the handle to release the soil.

CROWBARS

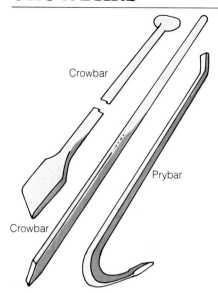

Crowbar

Prybar

Crowbar

The long crowbar, often called a prybar, is a specialty tool that is indispensable for prying out something heavy. The most versatile (therefore handiest) bar is ¾ inch in diameter, 5 feet in length, and about 18 pounds in weight. One end is pointed; the other end is often flattened to resemble a chisel blade.

This big crowbar was originally used by railroad men to move freight cars a few inches for coupling or uncoupling. Today, it is still used primarily for prying: You can remove large rocks buried deep in the ground by first digging out the soil from around them and then jamming the chisel end of the prybar under the rock. To increase your leverage, use another, smaller rock or a short length of 4 by 4 wood as a fulcrum.

The prybar is also very useful for digging postholes in hard or rocky ground. Use either end to break hard-clay soil or rocks at the bottom of the hole; then lift out the debris with a clamshell posthole digger or a straight shovel.

The prybar plus a fulcrum will lift out heavy, large-rootballed trees that must be removed for transplanting. The crowbar can also be used to punch holes in the ground for planting bean poles and for taking the temperature of a compost pile. To do the latter, plunge the bar into the center of the compost heap for about five minutes. Then grasp the end with one hand and remove it. The compost heap is the right temperature (about 140°) when the bar is not too hot to grasp but it is too hot to hold onto.

Crowbars normally are made from high-carbon steel, which gives them great strength. The tips rarely need any sharpening. If you do touch them up, use a coarse file. Never make them actually sharp or else they will bend if they strike rocks.

POWER CULTIVATORS

The *electric cultivator* is like a mini rotary tiller. The motor is above the blades at the end of a 4-foot shaft. Use this tool in soft soil—it is not powerful enough to turn new soil.

The *gas-powered cultivator* is a two-wheeled machine with a motor housed above the blades. It has several attachments, including a plow and cultivator tines. It can be used like a rotary tiller, although it is less powerful. If you have a large garden, this tool can be well worth buying.

Maintenance

The instruction manual for the particular tool covers its maintenance and repair. Follow its advice. However, all power cultivators should be wiped or hosed off after use and lightly oiled. Since oil attracts dirt, do not use an excessive amount.

Electric Cultivator

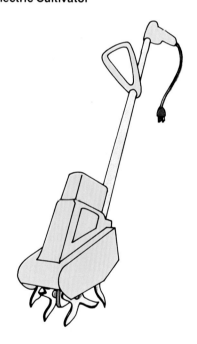

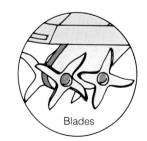

Blades

ROTARY TILLERS

A rotary tiller eliminates much of the gardening drudgery for homeowners with a quarter-acre or more. It does in minutes what normally takes hours with a shovel or hand cultivator. And it can be used year-round: In early spring, use it to turn under a crop of soil-enriching rye grass, then use it to prepare the garden seedbed; throughout the summer, use it as a cultivator; in the late fall, use it to mulch all crop residue; and in the winter, use it with a snowplow or snow-blower attachment to clear your driveway and walks.

There are basically two types of rotary tillers: (1) those with the tines in front of the wheels and (2) those with the tines behind the wheels. Both can perform a variety of functions, depending on what attachments are available with each model.

Front-tine tillers are cheaper than rear-tine tillers. However, they are chiefly for light to medium-duty garden tilling. They are used primarily in vegetable and flower beds that have been tilled before and have soft, smooth, and well-prepared soil. But front-tine tillers are very difficult to use if the ground is hard, rocky, or full of weeds. Since the tiller blades are linked to the engine by chains or drive belts and the machine is pulled forward by the action of the blades, when the tines hit hard ground, the tiller may go out of control and leap about. Further, to maintain control of the tiller, you must walk behind it; therefore the freshly turned ground will be compacted again—by the wheels and by your feet. Nevertheless, front-tine tillers are the most widely sold type and will work beautifully if your task is to rework soil that already has been tilled.

Rear-tine tillers, on the other hand, are heavier and are used for breaking ground that has been compacted by walking since the previous cultivation, that contains rocks and sticks, or that has other similar problems. Rear-mounted tines tend to dig down, literally pulling themselves into the soil; front-tine tillers may crawl up and out of hard ground. As a general rule, the heavier the tiller is, the less effort it requires of the operator and the better job it does.

To operate this tiller, keep the wheels on similar-textured soil (i.e., cultivated or uncultivated). Don't make the first pass across the soil too deep. Follow it with a second pass that's near but not right next to the first pass. This ensures that both wheels are on firm ground at all times. Make a third pass between and overlapping the first two, keeping both wheels on softened soil. This will make it easy for you to steer. Be sure to disengage the tiller when turning.

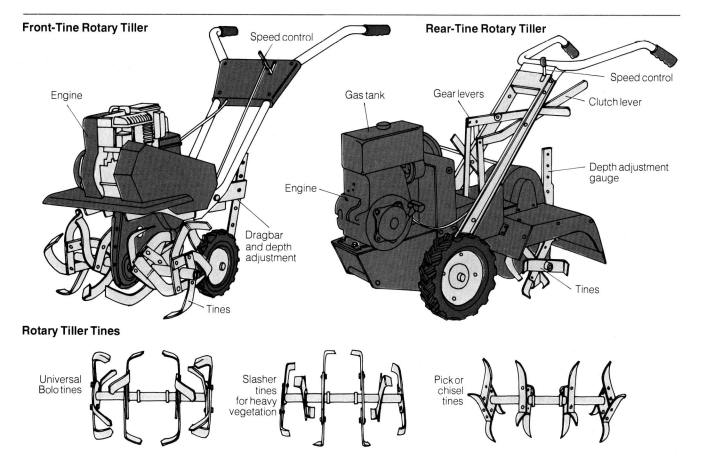

Front-Tine Rotary Tiller

Speed control

Engine

Dragbar and depth adjustment

Tines

Rear-Tine Rotary Tiller

Gas tank

Gear levers

Speed control

Clutch lever

Depth adjustment gauge

Engine

Tines

Rotary Tiller Tines

Universal Bolo tines

Slasher tines for heavy vegetation

Pick or chisel tines

How to Select a Tiller

Before buying a tiller, first consider whether your garden is large enough to justify the expense. If it is, then think about which type to choose. If your garden is less than a quarter-acre, a small power cultivator may do (see page 24). If your garden is a quarter-acre to a half-acre, you may need only a front-tine tiller. If you're tilling for the first time, you may want to rent a more powerful, rear-tine tiller to do the initial groundbreaking. Then, for future use, you can purchase the front-tine tiller. If you can afford it, however, consider buying a rear-tine tiller; it is heavier and more stable. Borrow a neighbor's tiller, or rent several and experiment with them. Especially if cost is an important factor, you may decide that renting makes more sense than buying, and it is always a good way to familiarize yourself with equipment.

Next, decide which attachments you need. If you live in heavy-snow country, a snowblower or at least a dozer blade could be worth every penny you spend. Make sure the tillers you evaluate offer the options you need.

Tines

Basic types of tines available for tillers are:
Bolo tines. These normally come with

the tiller. They have broad, heavy-duty blades that both dig and mulch. They are designed for a minimum of clogging.

Pick and chisel tines. These have medium-length, slightly curved blades that are designed primarily for working up hard, rocky ground. They tend to clog easily in vegetation.

Slasher tines. These have short, sharp points and are made to cut through thick vegetation and into soft ground. They need to be kept sharp to work efficiently.

Operating the Tiller

When you're tilling, the moisture of the ground is extremely important, especially if the soil is compacted or if it has never been tilled before. When the soil gets dry, it gets very hard; if it's too hard, the tiller may not be able to do more than scrape away at the first couple of inches. And if the soil is too wet, the tiller will form clods. Later, the sun dries these clods and they become like rocks, which can ruin the soil until the next winter's weather softens them again. If your soil is compacted or has never been tilled before, water it for several hours three or four days before tilling. Then check to see whether the soil has drained enough to be tilled: Turn a clod over with a shovel, pick up a handful of moist soil from the bottom of the shovel

hole, and squeeze the soil into a ball. It should be easy to break apart the ball with one finger. If it dents rather than breaks, the soil is still too moist to till.

Before tilling new ground, cut the weeds. If you try tilling through high or freshly cut weeds, they will wrap around the tines and tangle. If the weather is warm and dry, cut the weeds with a lawn mower or swing blade two or three days before tilling. If the weather is overcast or rainy, cut the weeds a couple of weeks before tilling. This gives the cut weeds time to dry and to soften via decomposition. Then the tiller can break the weeds apart rather than winding them up around itself.

Rotary tillers are dangerous—it's very important to keep your feet away from the tines and to stay in control of the machine at all times. This means: (1) having a tiller big enough for the job you're doing and (2) not going too fast. Rear-tine tillers are safer to use in the lower gears. Front-tine tillers are safer to use if you weigh down the depth bar by pushing down on the handlebars. The more you let go of the weight on the tines, the more the tiller has a tendency to run away from you.

Despite their size and weight, even large tillers can be operated by the average adult. Both front and rear-tine tillers may buck and gyrate while tilling. If you try

Operating Rotary Tillers

When operating a front-tine rotary tiller, walk behind it in order to control the machine.

With a rear-tine rotary tiller, walk beside it to guide the machine, but avoid walking over freshly tilled soil.

using physical strength to control either type, you will soon exhaust yourself. Instead, stay relaxed and let the tiller jump when it hits something hard; then guide it back on track.

Gyrating occurs most commonly when new ground is first tilled. Don't try to dig more than two or three inches deep the first time over the soil or sod. Make two or three passes, at right angles to each other if possible, and set the machine to dig deeper on each pass. Pushing down on the handlebars allows you to control how big a bite the tiller takes.

All tillers tend to walk forward. The self-driven, rear-end types drive themselves forward by the action of the tines, but even those that have motor drive to the wheels will move forward on their own. To keep them from running away, bear down hard on the handlebars, quickly reduce power by closing the throttle, or depress the clutch. Many rear-tine tillers have a reverse gear. In small gardens, these tillers can be operated in reverse on every other row; thus you go forward on one row, move over a little bit, and move in reverse in the next row. This saves you from having to make turns, which—with the large tillers—are difficult to do, especially if you're working next to a garage or fence.

Maintenance

Cleaning
To clean tillers, wipe the motor down thoroughly with a dry rag after each use, and clean carefully around the openings for gas and oil. Clear any debris away from the cooling fins on the engine. You don't have to clean the digging tines after each use unless they have a build-up of wet soil.

However, a tiller's digging tines do need frequent attention if they are cultivating tall growth. Both during operation and before storage, check periodically to make sure that vegetation is not wrapped around the tines and that soil has not built up. If you find either of these situations, first shut down the engine. Then remove the spark plug wire from the plug, making sure that it can't snap back and touch the plug. Remove all dirt and any debris that is wrapped around the axle of the tines or the tines themselves.

Sharpening
If the tines need sharpening, remove them according to instructions in the owner's manual, and touch the blades up with a small- or medium-size (6- to 10-inch) bastard mill file. The tines will probably be too worn for you to see the original sharpening bevel. File each tine's blade at a steep angle (70 to 80 degrees)—keeping lots of metal behind the edge gives the blade more strength. Don't make it actually sharp or else it will be nicked by the first rock you hit. If the blades are severely worn, they will not cut as deeply or efficiently as they should. Replace them.

Engine Care
As with all gas-powered machines, the tiller's engine needs to be regularly maintained and tuned (see pages 77-86).

Before putting your tiller away for the winter, follow the steps outlined in "Storing and Winterizing Power Equipment," page 13.

Sharpening Rotary Tiller Tines

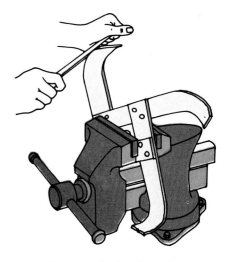

Place each tine in a vise and sharpen each blade at a steep 70–80° angle. You don't want to make the blade sharp. You just want to approximate the original bevel.

RAKES

Garden Rakes

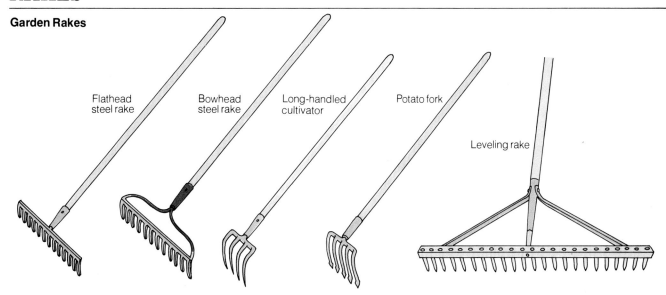

Flathead steel rake   Bowhead steel rake   Long-handled cultivator   Potato fork   Leveling rake

A good gardener needs two rakes: (1) a steel garden rake and (2) a lawn rake. A steel garden rake has many uses, but raking a lawn isn't one of them. The stiff tines dig into the grass instead of just sliding over it, and they quickly get clogged with leaves.

Garden Rakes

The garden rake comes in flathead or bowhead styles. Gardeners commonly use it to break up clods of dirt when preparing a seedbed for planting. Once the soil is pulverized, the flathead rake can be turned over to level and smooth the soil. Some gardeners also use this rake for thinning vegetables (e.g., radishes). A garden rake's quality is determined largely by the quality of steel in the rake head. Good rakes are made with high-carbon steel; the cheapest varieties may be of cast iron. A few high-quality rakes have a forged socket that connects the handle to the rake head. In some of these, the teeth are individually inserted through the head for even greater strength. But for the most part, steel garden rakes are made with tang-and-ferrule construction. When you choose a garden rake, make sure the head is firmly attached to the handle. Don't buy a garden rake with a head that wiggles—the head is bound to fall out when you use it.

Flathead Steel Rake

All flathead steel garden rakes have very similar designs: The head is about 15 inches wide. The 12 to 15 teeth are straight, or nearly so, and about 2½ inches long. The handles are 54 to 60 inches long. Often lighter and smaller than the bowhead rake, the flathead is good for doing fine cultivating or for finishing a seedbed. You can use it to work the surface soil to a very smooth, fine texture. Then, by simply

turning it over, you can do additional smoothing with the flat side. Its disadvantage is that the head is relatively weak and can break if you use it on heavy material.

Bowhead Steel Rake

The bowhead steel garden rake is named after the two tangs, which resemble a drawn bow, that hold the head away from the handle end. When in use, therefore, this rake has a little more spring action than the flathead rake. Some gardeners feel that this action reduces the strain that comes with extensive use. The bowhead is stronger and sometimes heavier than the flathead rake, and its longer handle and wider head tend to make it larger. Use it for leveling soil, raking heavy material, or spacing seeds in a prepared seedbed. To accomplish the last task, place the rake handle on the surface of the bed with the tines facing upward. Press the handle lightly into the soil. Then, using the head of the rake, press the tines lightly into this line. The small impressions (holes) from the tines are usually spaced about 1 inch apart. Place the seeds in these holes.

Long-Handled Cultivator

Although the long-handled cultivator is not really a rake, it is used for much the same purpose as the garden rake. It breaks up clods of soil and stirs the ground more deeply than a rake can. The lightweight cultivators are very good for raking leaves in flower beds when you have to work in close around plants. Hand cultivators have three tines (see page 33), but this cultivator has four or five. Its tines also are up to 5 inches longer, and they curve sharply for deeper cultivating.

Potato Fork

A potato fork, which is used for harvesting potatoes, resembles a large, heavy-duty cultivator. Landscapers sometimes buy

these forks and saw the tines off to about 4 inches. This makes a very coarse rake that does a quick (though not very thorough) job of cleaning. It's handy for cleaning very large areas, leveling a lot of soil quickly, or unloading coarse material from a truck or trailer.

Leveling Rake

The leveling rake is much like the antique hay rake. Its wooden head is broad (25 to 30 inches) and flat, and about 25 wooden pegs inserted in it function as teeth. These teeth, each nearly 4 inches long, will readily break up large, soft clumps of dirt in a freshly spaded garden. The rake can then be turned over to smooth and level the planting site. The wide head is normally braced with wood or metal stays that run from the head to the handle. Rental shops carry this rake, but in aluminum rather than wood. It is most commonly used for putting in a new lawn.

Lawn Rakes

Lawn rakes have fanlike, dull, springy teeth. These rakes are designed to glide over the grass so that they can remove clippings or leaves without catching in the sod. Lawn rakes commonly are made of steel, bamboo, or polypropylene (the last two don't rust).

Lawn rakes work most efficiently when handled like a broom—use a sweeping motion rather than a raking action.

Steel-Tine Rakes

Unlike the wire tines that characterize leaf rakes, steel-tine lawn rakes have flat tines. These flat tines vary considerably in steel quality. This quality can't really be determined simply by looking at the rake, but price gives one indication. The tines on a good steel lawn rake are made of spring steel; they will snap back into position

Using a Garden Rake

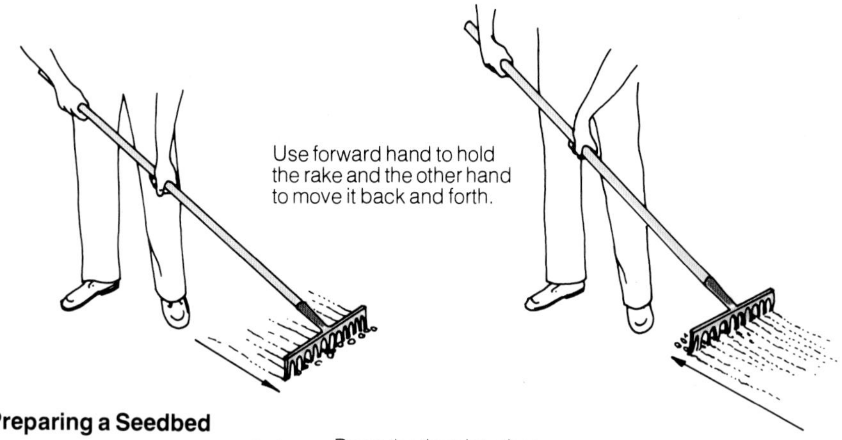

Use forward hand to hold the rake and the other hand to move it back and forth.

Preparing a Seedbed

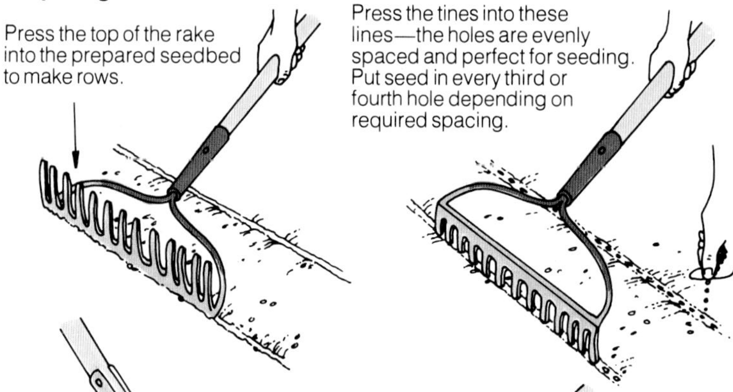

Press the top of the rake into the prepared seedbed to make rows.

Press the tines into these lines—the holes are evenly spaced and perfect for seeding. Put seed in every third or fourth hole depending on required spacing.

Lawn Rakes

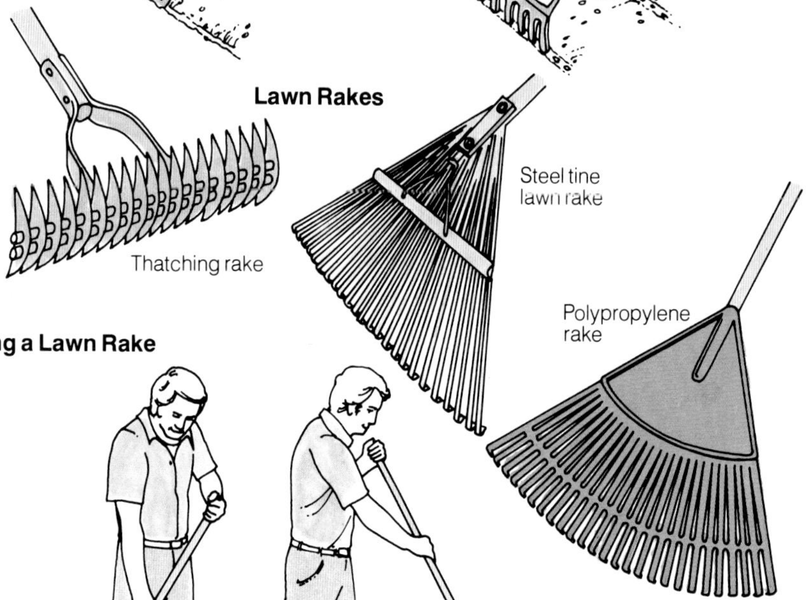

Thatching rake

Steel tine lawn rake

Polypropylene rake

Using a Lawn Rake

Lawn rakes work best when used like a broom. Use a sweeping rather than a pulling motion.

even when severely bent. Cheaper rakes, however, will stay bent. You can straighten the tine with a pair of pliers, but it will be weak at that point and may bend again. In addition to the problem of bending tines, this type of lawn rake requires more rust-preventive care than others.

Bamboo Rakes

Because bamboo rakes are made of cheap materials, they are relatively inexpensive. When one finally does wear out or break, you can replace it without making a big dent in your budget. To keep the tines flexible (particularly if your climate is arid), every two or three months soak the rake head overnight in a tray of soapy water. Be sure to soak it before using it in the summer.

Polypropylene Rakes

Polypropylene rakes used to be made quite poorly, but their improved construction out of stronger, new materials has caused their popularity to grow. They don't rust like metal rakes, and they don't become brittle and frayed like bamboo rakes. Look for good reinforcement across the tines and around the area where the head attaches to the handle. The heavy-duty models are most durable and are worth buying even if your lawn is small.

Thatching Rake

The thatching rake is a specialty tool for clearing lawns of the matted grass that smothers new lawn growth. The 15-inch-wide head has 20 or more curved cutting edges that pull and slide through the matted grass. Some models have heads that adjust to different angles, according to your height. Another model has teeth that move back and forth: When you pull, the teeth lock in place and bite into the thatch; when you push, the teeth roll up under the head to clear themselves.

Leaf Rakes

Leaf rakes have steel *wire* tines. Do not use these rakes on your lawn; the wire tines will tear the grass. However, you can use it anywhere else. Use a sweeping motion, as with lawn rakes.

Maintenance

It's easy to maintain rakes: Keep them clean, dry, and stored indoors. Clean your metal rakes as you would a hoe (see page 32), being careful to remove dirt from the area around tang-and-ferrule fittings. On lawn rakes, straighten bent steel tines with pliers. Never sharpen the tines on either garden or lawn rakes. If you put a rake on the ground after using it, be sure to point the tines downward so that you don't step on them. As with all your tools, remember to put your rakes away when you finish with them.

BLOWERS

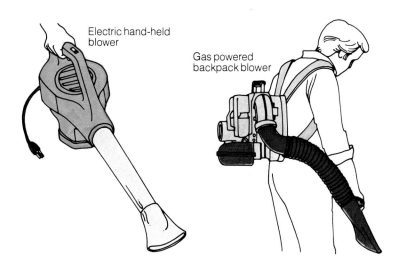

Electric hand-held blower

Gas powered backpack blower

Blowers first came about when home gardeners tinkered with power sprayers by emptying the mixing tank and using a blast of air to move leaves and debris. As blower owners have since discovered, the blower is not a one-season tool. In winter, it can be used to remove light snow from cars and walkways. During the rest of the year, it can be used to blow water from tennis courts, walkways around swimming pools, and rain gutters and to blow both wet and dry leaves into piles or wind rows for bagging or mulching. One landscaper declares that the blower is his single most valuable piece of equipment; it saves more time in commercial maintenance than any other tool.

Gas vs. Electric. Blowers come with either electric or gas-powered engines. The electric blower is limited by the length of the cord and the possibility of becoming entangled in shrubbery, but it has the advantages of instant power, relative quietness, and no fussing with fuel mixing or engine maintenance. However, electric blowers offer a smaller range of power options than do gas-powered blowers.

Gas-powered blowers range from the small, two-cycle-engine, hand-held or backpack models to the larger, four-cycle-engine, wheeled models that are used for large estates or small orchards. Their main advantage is that they allow unrestricted movement.

To determine what type of blower to buy, consider: How much of the year will you need it for? What size is your grounds? What is the weight of the debris to be blown? And what size and weight equipment can you use comfortably?

Air Speed. Blowers generally are rated by the air speed or air volume they develop. Air speed, which normally is stamped on the engine, ranges from 100 to 250 miles

per hour. Blowers with high air-speeds are for moving large amounts of debris quickly; those with low air-speeds are excellent for clearing leaves without disturbing bark mulch or for blowing leaves away from newly seeded lawns.

The greater the air speed, the heavier the engine. Small hand-held blowers usually weigh 10 pounds or less; backpack models range from 15 to 30 pounds; and the wheeled models, which are not self-powered, weigh from 200 to 250 pounds.

On many models, you can adjust the air velocity. This is usually done by varying the engine speed with a throttle built into the air hose or by adjusting air vanes in the hose.

On some models, the air stream can be reversed to draw leaves and other light materials into attached bags.

Safety. Safety precautions must be followed when using blowers. Keep your hands away from hot mufflers; wear ear and eye protectors, as required; and never direct the air stream at other people or at animals. Ear protectors are commonly needed if you're using the noisier gas-powered models. You don't need protective goggles for general snow or leaf removal, but you do when working in dusty conditions or in tight corners where sticks or small stones may be stirred up.

Maintenance

Consult your owner's manual for tips on cleaning.

The electric models require only minimal engine maintenance. If an electric engine does malfunction, take it to a qualified repairperson. For gas engines, follow the maintenance and tune-up steps for either the two-cycle or four-cycle engines (see pages 77–86).

SHREDDERS AND COMPOSTERS

Composting means turning waste material into a rich growing medium. The compost is a natural fertilizer that conditions the soil. You can find compost material everywhere: Leaves, grass and pruning clippings, old straw, manure, egg shells, and vegetable waste from the kitchen. But in order for the composting process to be efficient (i.e., to facilitate the bacteriological breakdown of plants), the material must first be chopped into fine pieces.

There are several ways to shred plant waste for compost: Use a lawn mower to shred leaves while they lie on the lawn; use a rotary tiller to chop and turn crop wastes directly into the soil; or, most efficiently, use a shredder.

Shredders

Most shredders are similar in design. There is a hopper on top in which to dump loose material, and a side opening through which to feed pruning clippings and small branches. Shredders differ primarily according to the size of the hopper, the size and type of the cutting devices, and the power of the engine.

The *hammer mill method* is most common for shredding materials of small to average size. Rows of free-swinging, short lengths of metal are fixed to a drive shaft that flails the plant material into small pieces.

The material is held in place near the shredding devices by a metal screen with holes about ¾ inch in diameter (in the standard version). When the hammer mills have broken the material down far enough, the material passes through these screen holes. Some manufacturers offer a wide choice of screens, with holes ranging from ⅛ inch up to 2 inches so that the user can vary the size of shredded material. Most models also have a roller-bar system that's used instead of the screens for handling wet or green material that doesn't pass through the screen holes easily.

Once the material is cut, it is thrown out a chute on the shredder's bottom or side. Some models come with a pan to catch the debris; others provide bags. In both cases, the purpose of the container is to move the shredded vegetation to the compost pile or to the garden for mulch.

Selecting a Shredder

Shredders come in both electric and gas-operated versions. In deciding which to buy, consider how far from a power source you must work. Gas models can be taken anywhere, even into the woods to shred a pickup's load of fall leaves; electric shredders must stay within reach of the nearest electric outlet. Engine sizes range from 3 to 8 horsepower. Obviously, the larger the

Parts of a Shredder

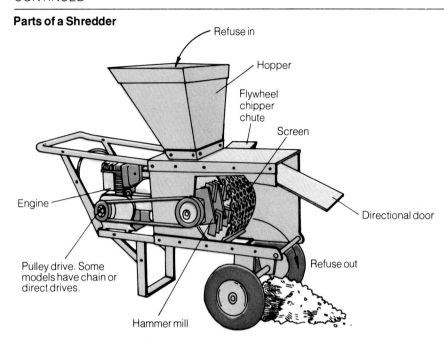

Refuse in

Hopper

Flywheel chipper chute

Screen

Engine

Directional door

Pulley drive. Some models have chain or direct drives.

Refuse out

Hammer mill

engine, the heavier the material it will handle—but the cost also increases proportionally.

Better shredders are built of 12- to 16-gauge steel; less expensive ones are made of sheet metal. Steel has the advantage of greater strength and durability.

Screens should be readily accessible so that you can change them according to the size of compost desired, or remove them when they get clogged. If you live in a wet climate, be sure to get a model with roller bars in addition to the screens.

Safety Measures
☐ Always wear protective goggles when working around a shredder.
☐ Never push material down the hopper with your hand. Use a stick.
☐ Do not let children feed the shredder or even play nearby when it is operating.
☐ Always unplug the power cord on an electric shredder before attempting to clear a jam.
☐ Remove the wire from the spark plug on gas-operated machines before attempting to clear a jam. Make sure the plug wire

will not fall back against the plug.
☐ Know how to turn the machine off quickly—you never know when this may be important.

Maintenance
Follow the manufacturer's recommendations for cleaning, sharpening, and lubricating. In general, cleaning involves washing out the hopper to remove the residue and keeping the screens unclogged.

Check the hammer mills, or steel flails, at least once a year (more often if they are used extensively). If any are broken, replace them.

Gas-operated shredders require routine engine maintenance. Virtually all shredders use a four-cycle engine, so the oil needs to be changed about every 25 operating hours. Use a 30-weight oil or whatever the manufacturer recommends. Consult the owner's manual and follow the engine maintenance and tune-up guidelines on pages 77–86.

If the shredding devices don't work but the engine does, the problem probably lies with the clutch or the belt. Check the owner's manual for trouble-shooting advice. If the problem isn't something you can handle comfortably, take the shredder to a competent repair shop or to your dealer.

Composters
Once the material has been shredded, the next step is to turn it into compost. The most effective way to do this is in a composter (compost container), which keeps the pile of material orderly and capable of retaining the heat generated by the bacteriological breakdown process.

Types of Composters
The advantage of using a compost container is that, unlike a pile in the open air, it retains heat. Composters also provide adequate air holes and access for shoveling. You may want three composters in which to keep piles that are in various stages of the process. If you like to build, try making the three adjoining bins described in ORTHO's *Wood Projects for the Garden.*

You can buy a commercially available composter that's made from heavy plastic with ventilation holes on the sides. The top is hinged for easy loading and the panels on the side slide up to shovel out compost at the bottom. These bins are about 3 feet high and 3 feet in diameter.

You can also buy the rotating-drum-type composter. It resembles a 55-gallon oil drum suspended on its side. A hinged door provides access for filling and a crank lets you tumble the material inside to give it oxygen.

Compost Bins

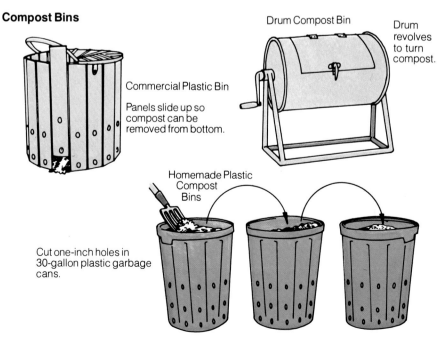

Commercial Plastic Bin

Panels slide up so compost can be removed from bottom.

Drum Compost Bin

Drum revolves to turn compost.

Homemade Plastic Compost Bins

Cut one-inch holes in 30-gallon plastic garbage cans.

HOES

Types of Hoes

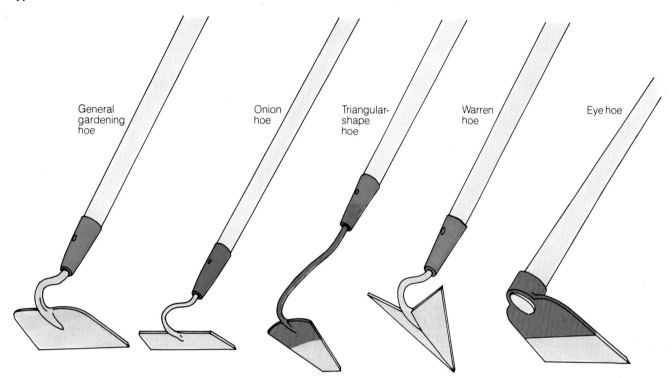

General gardening hoe

Onion hoe

Triangular-shape hoe

Warren hoe

Eye hoe

Hoes are designed to accomplish two major tasks: (1) cultivation (chopping, loosening, and moving light soil) and (2) weeding (cutting off weeds at or just below the soil surface). There is the standard garden hoe, which is used primarily for cultivation, and there is the scuffle hoe, which is used only for cutting off small weeds. These hoes vary greatly in style.

Hoes, like shovels, spades, and forks, are usually made with a solid forged socket or with a tang-and-ferrule construction (see page 15). A third style, often found on heavy-duty hoes, has an "eye" at the top of the blade, with a mattocklike handle fitted through the eye. Follow the rule that applies to all your tools: Select the one with the strongest construction possible.

Handles range in length from 50 to 60 inches; yours should be long enough to let you work without having to bend unduly. As for blades, the sizes vary considerably. Some are sharpened only on the bottom, some on all three sides, and some not at all. The following descriptions will help you decide which type to buy. Also consider your garden's size and type: For heavy or rocky soil, you'll need a hoe that's big enough to do the job; for a small border garden, a narrow-blade or pointed hoe will be more suitable; for a specific weeding problem that can't be solved by a standard garden hoe, consider a scuffle hoe. Try out your neighbor's hoes to see which do best in your own garden.

Types of Hoes

General Gardening Hoe
The general gardening hoe is the one found in the toolsheds of most gardeners. Because the blade is slightly angled, it slips just beneath the soil to cut weeds on each downward stroke. The blade emerges from the end of a gooseneck-shape tang or socket. It usually has a beveled cutting edge on the outer side, and is between 5 and 7 inches wide. The heavier your soil, the heavier your hoe should be.

Onion Hoe
The onion hoe has a broader head (about 7 inches by 2 inches). The blade is sharpened on the sides as well as on the bottom. The broad head is designed for working between onion rows, but when turned on edge it can weed and cultivate in the tight spaces between onions or other bulb-type plants.

Triangular-Shape Hoe
The triangular-shape hoe has an arrow-shaped head; the tapered end with its flat tip is better than the standard hoe for breaking into stubborn soil. This hoe is also excellent for weeding: The blade breaks deeply into the soil around the roots of the weed and then jerks out the entire plant rather than just cutting off the portion above ground. It is also useful for weeding or cultivating in tight spots. The flat tip is sharpened like any other hoe.

Warren Hoe
The Warren hoe, however, has a pointed tip and does not need to be sharpened. This hoe was developed to make furrows for vegetables, irrigation furrows, and trenches for planting sets or large seeds. After planting, flip the hoe over and pull the two points along either side of the furrow to cover the sets or seeds. Some gardeners try to use the Warren hoe as a weeding tool, but its construction makes it fairly ineffective for this purpose. The pointed tip must be aimed at a weed very directly, or else the tip will just slide past it. And the severe angle of the blade in relation to the handle means that you must bend quite low in order to use it properly. However, it is good for its intended purpose—making furrows.

Eye Hoe
The eye hoe is designed to tackle big jobs and to last a lifetime. The head is fitted directly onto the handle, which flares at one end so that it won't come off. The blades vary in size according to the requirements of the job. There are standard-size cultivating blades (7½ inches by 6¾ inches); blades for chopping weeds and light brush (4 inches by 7 inches); and other blades, the largest of which is the specialized grape hoe that's used widely in California vineyards (8 inches by 7 inches).

Types of Scuffle Hoes

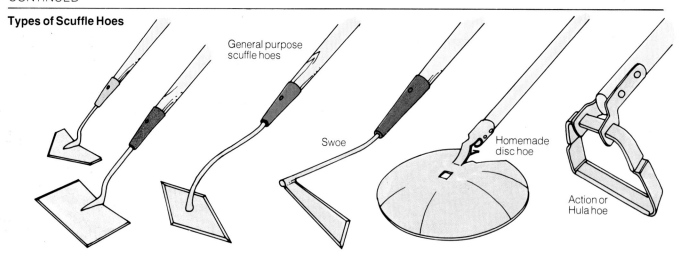

General purpose scuffle hoes

Swoe

Homemade disc hoe

Action or Hula hoe

Scuffle Hoe
The scuffle hoe is used primarily for weeding and occasionally for tilling. However, if your garden is already well tilled and your main task is keeping small weeds from becoming established, the scuffle hoe makes a good second hoe. It generally has a flat blade that rests parallel to the ground and is beveled both on the front and the back. To cut weeds with a standard hoe, you move the blade in one direction, but with a scuffle hoe you move the blade back and forth. You can also turn this hoe over and use it to cultivate the soil or to edge a border. Since scuffle hoes are all designed to accomplish the same thing, which one you choose is largely a matter of preference. Keep the blades sharp and out of rocky or heavy-clay soils.

The *action hoe*, also called a *hula hoe*, is so named because the blade moves about ½ inch each way when it's either pushed or pulled. The slight movement adjusts the blade angle so that it cuts down at the roots of weeds.

The *disc hoe* is fixed in one position to ride parallel to the ground whether it is pushed or pulled. Both the front and back have notches to catch and cut larger weeds. All four sides are sharp. Run this hoe back and forth through weeds, just beneath the soil surface.

The *swoe* is a cross between a standard hoe and a scuffle hoe. Made of stainless steel, it is about 2 inches wide at the cutting end, narrowing to about 1 inch near the handle. Since the blade is sharp on all three edges, it will cut when pulled or pushed to either side.

The *diamond-shape scuffle hoe* is excellent for working in tight places, such as in border gardens. The hoe is about 2 inches wide in the center, narrowing down to about ½ inch at each end. All the edges are sharp. It is convenient to use for cultivating under a mulch, such as bark.

Maintenance

Cleaning
The first thing is to keep your hoe clean. If it has a tang-and-ferrule construction, make sure the ferrule fits tightly around the handle end so that soil doesn't get in; eventually, soil would rot the wood and cause the tang to fall out.

Sharpening
Sharpen your hoe at regular intervals. Place it horizontally in a vise, with the blade up. The bevel, which is usually on the side, ranges anywhere from a 45-degree angle for cutting weeds to an 85-degree angle for working hard ground. Use a 10- to 14-inch bastard mill file, and place it on the blade at the same angle as the bevel. Push the file down and away from you in one motion; the file should traverse the width of the blade on each stroke. At the end of the stroke, lift the file, bring it back to the corner edge nearest you, and repeat the cycle. Maintain even and constant pressure on each stroke; filing one spot excessively will cause that area to be cupped.

When you finish, place the file flat against the inside (nonbeveled) edge of the hoe and make a few strokes to remove any metal burrs (fine metal pieces) caused by the filing.

Storing
It's particularly important to store your hoe properly. Otherwise, you run two major risks: (1) if you leave the hoe outdoors at the mercy of the elements, the handle may get dry rot and (2) if the hoe is left lying on the ground with the blade up, you may step on it—with very unpleasant results.

Sharpening a Hoe

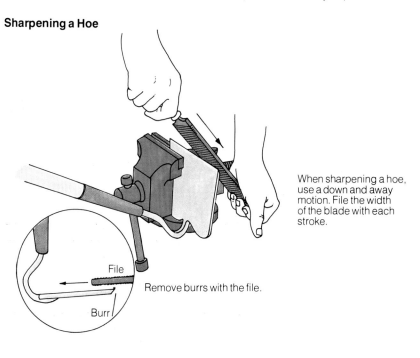

When sharpening a hoe, use a down and away motion. File the width of the blade with each stroke.

File

Remove burrs with the file.

Burr

HAND CULTIVATORS AND WEEDERS

Cultivating with a Hoe

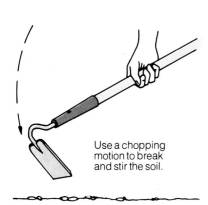

Use a chopping motion to break and stir the soil.

Weeding with a Hoe

Pull the hoe toward you. . .

cutting off the plant just below ground level.

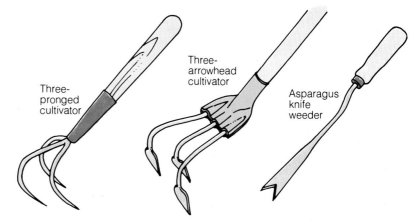

Three-pronged cultivator

Three-arrowhead cultivator

Asparagus knife weeder

Cultivators are generally used to aerate the soil or to weed close in to plants. In good garden soils they are used instead of a hoe, since a hoe is best in harder, heavier soils. Hand cultivators have short handles to accommodate gardeners who work on their knees in flower beds. They are usually constructed with the tang-and-ferrule system (see page 15). When examining quality, look for a comfortable handle and spring-steel tines or blades that resist bending.

Weeders are made to dig out weeds without removing chunks of your lawn. Remember to cut the weed below the surface or to expose the roots to the drying air.

Three-Pronged Cultivator
The three-pronged cultivator is used by many gardeners to incorporate materials into the soil, to loosen soil, and to do localized raking and weeding. The slender, spring-steel tines are moderately curved to allow you to work between 1 and 2 inches below the surface. The handle is either wood or bright-colored plastic, and it should be large enough to fit your hand comfortably.

Three-Arrowhead Cultivator
The three-arrowhead cultivator is designed almost exclusively for weeding alongside row crops in a vegetable garden; it has few other uses. The purpose of the three heads on this cultivator is to cover a large area on each stroke. Because the heads are angled sharply back toward the handle, they will work only 2 or 3 inches into the soil. On a good-quality tool, the tines are V-shaped on the inner side to slip through the soil better.

Asparagus Knife Weeder
This tool has a 9-inch steel shaft that flares on the end and is V-notched to hook and pry up weeds that have deep tap roots. Since the V is sharpened, it can cut roots well below the surface. The narrow shaft is used to pry the plant out of the ground without leaving a large hole. When this tool comes with a long handle for upright weeding, it is called a forked-shaft weeder.

Since this tool is used regularly for fairly heavy prying, choose one with a strong steel shaft. Some handles are made of wood; others are made of brightly colored plastic and are highly visible when left in the grass.

Maintenance
Keep all cultivators clean and lightly oiled. You don't have to sharpen the tines—they are self-sharpening. Because of the taper of the metal, normal wear keeps the ends sharp instead of rounding them. Since they are sharp, place them face-down whenever you put them on the ground. Short-handled cultivators, like trowels, are easy to lose in the garden. Choose specific places to put them, both during use and in storage.

Weeding

Dig deep to pry up tap root.

WEED AND BRUSH CUTTERS

Unlike hoes or other cultivators that remove or kill weeds, weed cutters are designed not to kill weeds but to make them shorter. Weed cutters are used primarily to control weeds along roadsides, in areas used for waste, and in unused fields. Basic tools used to control weeds and brush include the sickle, scythe, grass whip, swing blade, and brush cutter. They all have a sharp steel blade, but each is used differently. The most common weed cutters used by today's homeowners are the grass whip and swing blade. Brush cutters are used for chopping away heavy weeds, brambles, or light brush. Sickles and scythes are now used infrequently.

When buying one of these tools, look for high-quality steel. Although you can't determine the metal by looking at the blade, ask a salesperson to inform you of what material has been used. Quality-steel blades are hardened by a high percentage of carbon; they will hold an edge well and will resist nicking or cracking. Feel the difference by comparing the weight of cheap and expensive models.

Next, check that the blade is firmly fixed to the handle. It should not be loose or flimsy. The blade end should be set deep in the handle and held with two or more rivets.

The grass whip has a steel handle, but the swing blade has a wooden handle, which should be straight-grained ash or hickory.

Types of Cutters

Grass Whip
The grass whip is best used on grass or light weeds; heavier material may bend or damage it. Since it is made to be used with one hand, cut the weeds or grass by gaining a lot of momentum in a long swing and letting the power behind the swing cut the weeds for you. Handles come in varying lengths; try out a few different models to find one that suits your height. Since most blades are riveted to the steel handle, it is generally more practical to buy a new grass whip than to try replacing the blade.

Swing Blade
The swing blade is similar to the grass whip, but it is used on slightly heavier weeds. It generally has a straight wooden handle about the diameter of a broomstick. In comparison to the grass whip, the metal straps of the swing blade attach to both ends of the cutting blade, not just to one. Also, the cutting blade is thicker and stronger; the handle is thicker; and the construction is stronger. The swing blade is held in both hands and used the same way as a grass whip—with long, looping swings.

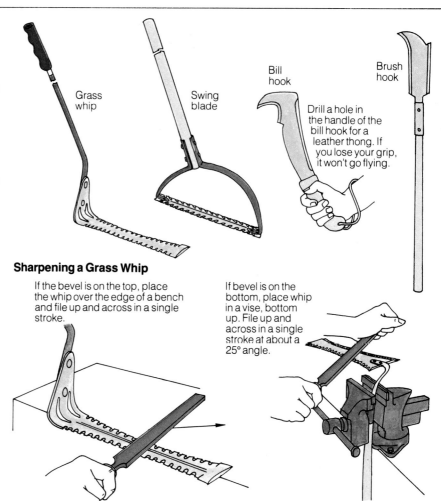

Sharpening a Grass Whip

If the bevel is on the top, place the whip over the edge of a bench and file up and across in a single stroke.

If bevel is on the bottom, place whip in a vise, bottom up. File up and across in a single stroke at about a 25° angle.

Drill a hole in the handle of the bill hook for a leather thong. If you lose your grip, it won't go flying.

Brush Cutters
The short-handled brush cutter is sometimes called a bill hook; those most commonly seen in this country are machetes. Its shorter handle enables it to make a small cutting arc and thus to provide a controlled swing. Thus it is good for working in close areas. However, in heavy thorny brambles, such as overgrown blackberry vines, you must first cut your way into the interior in order to reach the base of the plants.

For safety purposes, drill a hole in the end of the handle and loop a leather thong through it and around your wrist. This way if you lose your grip, the tool will not fly toward a bystander.

Brush cutters also come in long-handled versions to give you more reach.

Maintenance

Cleaning
After using weed cutters, wipe them clean and dry them. Apply a light coating of oil to protect them in storage.

Sharpening
Weed cutters need to be sharpened regularly, so keep an oval-shape whetstone handy. You can also use a smooth 8-inch mill file. Many gardeners keep the sharpening stone in their pocket so that the tools can have a perfect edge at all times. What is "perfect"? The blades should slice through the grass or weeds with very little drag.

Grass whips may have smooth or serrated cutting edges, and the bevel may be on the bottom or the top. Whether the edge is serrated or not, if the bevel is on the bottom, place the grass whip in a vise, bottom-side up, and file down and across each bevel in a single stroke. The bevel angle is usually about 25 degrees. Remove the burrs on the opposite side by running the file on the top side, making sure that it is held flat or parallel to that side.

If the bevel is on the top, place the grass whip bottom-side down on a bench, and let the edge to be sharpened hang over the bench slightly. With one hand, hold the whip securely; with the other, file from the heel toward the tip. When you are finished with the beveled side, remove any burrs on the unbeveled side.

WHEELBARROWS AND CARTS

If you don't have a wheelbarrow, you might not think you're missing anything. But once you get one, you won't know how you got along without it. Wheelbarrows simplify all your carrying chores; they can be loaded with leaves, rubbish, firewood, compost, children, or whatever will fit; and they can also be used for mixing (e.g., soils or cement).

Because wheelbarrows have one wheel rather than two, they are easier than carts to maneuver and to keep level on irregular ground—as long as you keep the weight of the load forward over the wheel. Carts, however, are better than wheelbarrows if your path is wide and level, and if you don't want to lift your loads. Also, a large, heavy-duty cart can accommodate larger loads than any wheelbarrow can.

The more durable heavy-duty wheelbarrows and carts have trays (bodies) made of steel and are painted or epoxy-enameled. One exception is the heavy-duty cart that is made of tubular steel with plywood sides and bottom. Some smaller and lighter wheelbarrows and carts are made of plastic.

Good wheelbarrows and carts have enclosed bearings in the wheels. Some of these are sealed and permanently lubricated. Others have a zerk fitting that must be greased with a grease gun once a year (more often in dusty areas).

Handles on the heavy-duty models are usually made of hardwood; on the lighter models they are made of tubular steel.

So many different sizes and shapes of wheelbarrows are available that making a choce might be difficult. But there's an easy way to choose: As long as you are reasonably fit, get the largest one you can afford. It's easier to take a single large load, particularly of light material (e.g., leaves or garden refuse), than it is to make two or three separate trips.

Types of Wheelbarrows and Carts

Light-Duty Steel Wheelbarrow
This wheelbarrow can carry light to moderate loads. Its tray, which is about 30 by 25 by 7 inches deep and holds up to 3 cubic feet, is made of one-piece steel with a baked epoxy enamel finish. The handlebars are made of tubular steel. The wheel has nylon bearings that do not need oiling.

Contractor's Wheelbarrow
This type works very well for both light and heavy-duty jobs because it is better balanced. The tray runs from 4½ to 5 cubic feet; on the larger models, it measures about 37 by 27 by 14 inches deep. The tray is available in three shapes: (1) square with a flat end (for working with loose materials, such as soil); (2) long and rounded (for mixing cement and pouring liquids); and (3) a combination of these two types.

The wheel is about 4 inches wide to support heavy loads in soft ground. Some models have sealed wheel bearings that need no greasing; others have a zerk fitting and require periodic greasing. The contractor's wheelbarrow is available with either a metal or a hardwood frame.

Heavy-Duty Cart
If you don't have a pickup or trailer, use this big cart to move large loads (e.g., bales of hay, garbage cans, or lumber). The box is made of ½-inch exterior plywood and measures about 28 by 48 by 15 inches deep. The plywood is stained to resist weathering. The framework is made of heavy steel tubing. The wheels are about 26 inches in diameter, with ball-bearing hubs.

Maintenance
Wheelbarrows and carts don't need much in the way of maintenance—basically just to be kept clean and free of rust. Rust can start whenever the enamel or paint on the tray is chipped, thus exposing the steel. If this happens, sand the steel clean. Then touch it up with a spray paint to protect the metal. Grease the wheels, if required, about once a year. If they begin to squeak, you have waited too long—some wear has occurred.

Never bounce wheelbarrows and carts over curbs or bumps; lower them down gently. Bouncing will quickly ruin the bearings.

Safety
You can injure your back by overloading a wheelbarrow. If a heavy wheelbarrow begins to topple, set it down immediately. Redistribute the load, keeping the weight over the front wheel.

Types of Wheelbarrows

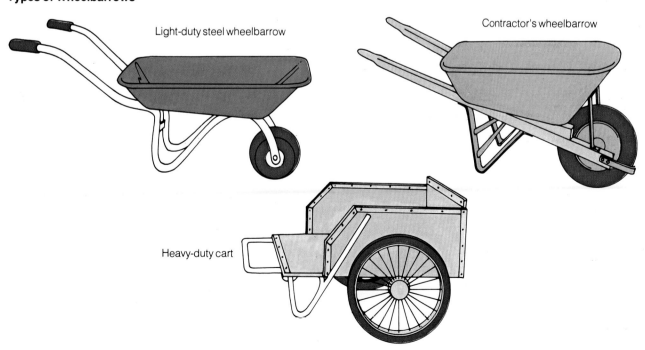

Light-duty steel wheelbarrow

Contractor's wheelbarrow

Heavy-duty cart

CARING FOR YOUR LAWN

Simplify the care of your lawn by selecting tools designed to make your job as easy as possible. Learn all about the features and maintenance requirements of the many types of mowers, trimmers, edgers, sweepers, and spreaders now available.

The care and feeding of a lawn can be quite an ordeal. There's the weekly mowing (as well as the raking, if you don't have a collection device). But mowing isn't the end of it—there's also trimming, edging, and weeding. Then there's the watering, with all the attendant worries about whether you're doing it too often or not often enough. And when you finally have the lawn in reasonable shape, you reward it with a shot of fertilizer, which just makes the grass grow faster and require more mowing, more trimming, more watering, and more feeding. In short, it's a vicious circle.

But if you have the right tools for the job, these tasks can be satisfying rather than dreary.

This chapter tells you about most of the tools involved in good lawn care, what to look for when you're buying a new piece of equipment, and how to maintain it so you get your money's worth.

Lawn Mowers

Many mowers are on the market, and analyzing your needs thoroughly will help you find the right one for you. You can choose from among push mowers, electric mowers, floating mowers, mower-mulchers, and many others.

When you select a new mower, first think about the size of your lawn. If it's small enough and you're in good enough shape, a push mower might be what you need. An electric power mower will do more and thus require less work, but it will only go as far as the cord will reach. And then there's

the ultimate—a riding mower or lawn tractor.

Consider the size of the engine and the width of the cutting swath. The size of the engine generally ranges from 3 to 4½ horsepower; professional models range up to 7 horsepower. The larger your lawn, the more powerful an engine you will need, particularly if you tend to wait until your grass gets fairly long before you mow it.

On most models, the width of the cutting swath makes the work go faster; it also means a heavier engine to manage and maintain, as well as a higher price. If your lawn mower has a narrow swath, you can make up the extra inch or two in a couple of passes.

Also think about what type of terrain you will be mowing. If the land is hilly, you may prefer a self-propelled mower, with powered wheels and cutting mechanism, over one that requires pushing. Be sure to check for features that will prevent the mower from "scalping" (cutting too close) a hilly part of the lawn.

Another decision involves the type of starting mechanism. Most gasoline-engine power mowers have pull-recoil starters. However, if this method doesn't appeal to you and you can afford something more expensive, consider a battery starter.

A few other things to look for are:
☐ Easy-to-adjust mower wheels for changing cutting heights.
☐ A deflector chute over the grass-discharge opening.
☐ A cast aluminum (preferably not steel) or heavy plastic housing around the blade.
☐ An automatic governor to keep the engine turning at a fairly constant speed.
☐ Electronic ignition in the engine.
☐ A compression release switch to make it easier to start the engine.
☐ Other accessories—for example, for mulching, shredding, and vacuuming—that are available on some models.

Of course, most of these features will add to the cost, so you must decide whether the benefits justify the investment.

 If your mower starts right up and runs well, mowing is more pleasant.

Trimming and edging around borders and trees makes your lawn look much neater. Descriptions of tools designed for this purpose begin on page 42.

Push Reel Mower

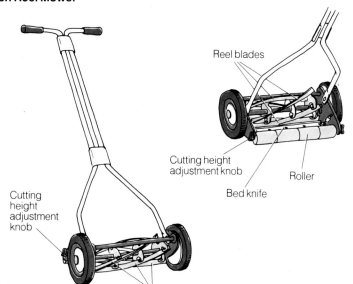

Reel blades

Cutting height
adjustment knob

Bed knife

Roller

Cutting
height
adjustment
knob

Reel blades

Power Reel Mower

Throttle

Clutch

Roller

Reel blades

Bed knife

Push Reel-Mowers

The push mower is the old, familiar stand-by. If your lawn is small consider the push mower. Properly maintained and sharpened, it will give you years of good, inexpensive service.

Push mowers have from five to eight spiral steel blades, which turn on a reel and catch the grass, slicing it against the fixed blade or bed knife. This scissorlike action provides a very fine cut, but the push mower operates well only on even ground with short to medium-length grass. It also requires careful maintenance.

The blades must be kept sharp and the mechanism must be adjusted so that each blade passes smoothly and evenly across the bed knife. When the blades are stopped, two of them should be touching the bed knife, one at either end. Rotate the

Adjusting the Bed Knife

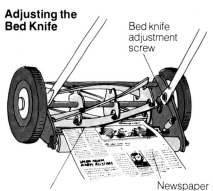

Bed knife
adjustment
screw

Newspaper

If knife is adjusted properly, each blade will cut the paper all the way across the bed knife.

reel, watching carefully to see that each blade touches the bed knife all the way across as it turns. The best way to check this is to put strips of paper between the reel and the bed knife; then turn the reel by hand and see whether the knife cuts the paper as it rotates. Adjust by raising or lowering the bed knife, as necessary.

Power Reel-Mowers

The same reel-type mower that you push is also available in a powered version. If your lawn is level and you want a manicured look, consider the fine-cutting reel mower. This is the one used by most professional lawn cutters for all fine lawns and many parks and golf fairways. The reel-mower blade makes a clean cut; in contrast, the rotary mower rips off the tops of the grass, leaving the remaining tips to turn brown.

Safety is another significant advantage. If rotary blades hit rocks or pipes, they may shatter and become flying missiles; reel blades, however, won't do this.

Power reel-mowers generally are driven by a four-cycle engine with 3½ to 4½ horsepower. Cutting swaths range from 16 to 20 inches. Some larger models are self-propelled, and some also have electric starters. Mowing heights generally range from ½ inch to 3 inches.

Professionals who use reel mowers often cut the lawn twice—once in one direction and then again at a right angle. This double cutting removes the ridges left by the wheels of the first cutting. If you choose this method, wait a bit in between cuttings to allow the grass blades to straighten up.

Rotary Mowers

This versatile mower allows you to cut almost anything within reason, including wet grass and weeds several feet tall (a reel mower can't handle these).

The rotary blade is easy to remove or replace when it is worn or cracked. You won't need to do this often, however; the blade will cut even when dull—the mower's tremendous speed simply rips the grass in half.

Most rotary mowers throw their clippings out the side; however, some throw them out the rear, others out the front. If no bag is attached to the mower to collect clippings, don't point the exit chute at a house, person, or animal; if the mower should throw a rock, a window might get broken or someone might get hurt. And rear-throw mowers must have a bag to catch the clippings; never operate these machines without one.

Battery-Powered Mower

This mower is quieter than the gasoline-powered version and is an excellent choice for use on smaller lawns (under 1,500 square feet). Under normal cutting conditions, the battery operates for about 45 minutes. It comes with a recharging unit that plugs into any 110-volt household outlet and starts electrically. The mower has a 16- to 18-inch cutting swath. Weighing around 50 pounds, it is lighter than some other types of mowers, which makes it a good choice if you don't have strong arms.

Electric Mower

The electric mower is a popular choice for

homeowners with small to medium-size lawns (under 4,000 square feet). Like the battery-powered mower, this one is relatively lightweight. It is also very easy to start and essentially maintenance free (see page 78). If a problem does develop, take the mower to a qualified repairperson.

Electric mowers have a 16 to 20-inch cutting swath and will operate on an extension cord, from 100 to 150 feet from an outlet. Determine your mowing pattern in advance to prevent running over the cord.

Economy Mower
This is the standard, no-frills mower that cuts thousands of lawns across the country. It has either a two-cycle or four-cycle engine of 3 to 4 horsepower, with a standard ignition system. It is not self-propelled—only the blade is powered, not the wheels. The cutting swath is 19 to 21 inches, and cutting heights generally range from 1½ to 3½ inches. The height is easy to adjust; just shift a small lever near each wheel. All models have a pull-recoil starter. Some newer machines may have a switch to release engine compression to make starting easier. Electric starters are available for similar mowers, but this adds to the cost.

Engine speed is controlled by a throttle on the handlebars near the operator's hand. The handlebars generally can be folded for convenient storage or transport.

Self-Propelled Mower
The self-propelled, electric-start mower is in the luxury class. Both wheels and blades are driven by 4 to 6-horsepower engines with up to four different walking speeds. For safety, the gear-driven wheels are engaged by a "deadman's clutch" on the handlebars, which stops the forward motion when released. Cutting swaths are 20 to 22 inches.

The electric start is provided by a small, rechargeable battery mounted near the engine. All such mowers also have a recoil starter, should the battery fail.

Most of these mowers now have a trouble-free, transistorized electronic ignition, which eliminates the breaker points and condenser used in standard electrical systems.

Engine speed is controlled either by a throttle on the handlebars or by a switch that offers high and medium speeds. Most of these models have an automatic choke and a governor to provide constant engine speed under varying grass conditions.

Mower-Mulcher
This is a relatively new type of mower on the market. It is similar to a standard mower, except that it has a special blade to cut grass and leaves into a fine powder. This powder is then blown back into the grass as a mulch, which saves you the trouble of raking or bagging. On most models, the grass clippings can be directed into a catch bag when the grass is too long or wet for effective mulching.

Mulchers also are available as accessories for some mower models and can be easily attached or removed when necessary.

Air-Cushion Mower
These mowers need no wheels, since they ride on a cushion of air. An impeller just below the engine pulls air down and out under the housing, thus lifting it. Since this rotary blade cuts the grass almost as finely as a mulcher and deposits it back in the lawn, there is no discharge chute.

Both electric and gas-powered models are available, with cutting swaths ranging from 15 to 20 inches. The mower floats about ¼ inch off the ground, and the cutting height is adjusted by raising or lowering the blade rather than the mower.

These low-profile mowers slip easily under low bushes and along borders and ride over the edge of downward slopes without scalping them.

Because they have no wheels, these mowers must be carried to and from the cutting site. Weights range from about 25 pounds for electric models up to around 40 for the gas-operated types. The mowers do not handle tall grass well and should not be run across dirt areas—dirt will be sucked into the machine and damage the blade.

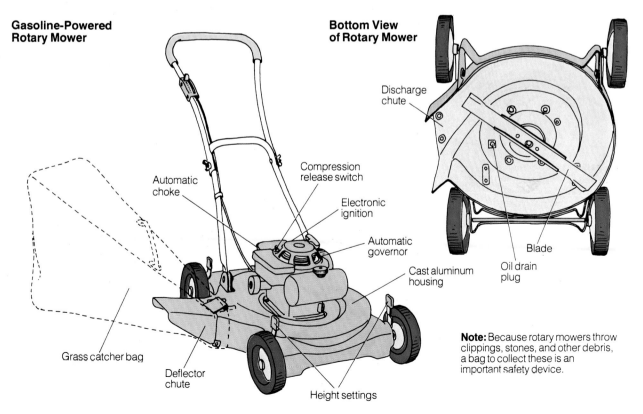

Gasoline-Powered Rotary Mower

Bottom View of Rotary Mower

Automatic choke

Compression release switch

Electronic ignition

Automatic governor

Cast aluminum housing

Discharge chute

Blade

Oil drain plug

Grass catcher bag

Deflector chute

Height settings

Note: Because rotary mowers throw clippings, stones, and other debris, a bag to collect these is an important safety device.

Maintenance

Cleaning

Push mowers. First scrape away the accumulated grass with a stick or a wire brush. Hose off the mower and then wipe down each blade and all metal parts with an oily rag.

Power mowers. Using a small stick, remove all grass and debris from between the cooling fins around the engine. If you don't, the engine will overheat and damage internal parts. Then, using a *clean* dry rag (an oily rag will attract more dirt), wipe down the engine and the housing. Be particularly careful to clean around the oil and gas openings (see page 89).

If the mower is already badly coated with oil and dirt, first wash it with hot, soapy water. Then hose it off and let it dry in the sun. Be careful not to let much water run around the spark plug—wipe it with a damp cloth instead of hosing it.

If the engine fails to start after you have washed it, remove the plug and wipe it with a clean, dry rag. Also wipe the inside of the hole. Then put a quarter-teaspoon of gasoline down the plug hole. Replace the plug and start the engine.

The underside of a power mower also needs regular cleaning, particularly when the mower is used to cut very green or damp grass. This grass will accumulate; when dry it can become as hard as cardboard, making it difficult to scrape off. On a rotary mower, the grass can also plug the blowhole for the clippings. To clean the underside, first pull the spark plug wire free from the plug to prevent it from starting accidentally if the blade turns. Then tip the rotary mower to the side and hose off all clippings from the underside of the housing, using a power nozzle. Do not allow the engine to get wet while it is hot; however, you can spray the bottom side of the mower without spraying the engine. Then let the mower sun-dry. To prevent grass clippings from sticking, try spraying the underside with a product that prevents food from sticking to frying pans.

Sharpening

Reel mowers. Most reel mowers are best sharpened by professionals to ensure even and accurate work.

Rotary mowers. A dull rotary-mower blade will cut grass, but it will leave it looking ragged. In addition, it may be out of balance, which will make the mower vibrate excessively and damage the engine. If either symptom appears, remove and sharpen the blade.

To remove a rotary blade for sharpening, follow these steps:

1. Run the tank nearly dry so that gasoline won't spill when you tip the mower on its side.

2. If your mower has an oil-bath filter, remove it.

3. *Always* remove the spark plug to guarantee that the engine won't start. If the spark plug wire were connected, the engine might start when you turned the blade to remove it. Tuck the wire back so it won't fall forward and rest against the plug.

4. With an adjustable wrench, loosen the nut holding the blade, and remove the blade. You may have to block the blade with a piece of scrap wood to keep it from turning with the wrench.

Most blades have two small shear pins set in them. These keep the blade from turning under the holding nut and protect the engine. If the blade hits something unmovable, the pins shear off and the blade stops, but the engine keeps running. (If it stopped abruptly, it could be damaged.) These pins will come out when you remove the blade; be careful to keep track of them so you can return them to their proper place later on.

5. Place the blade in a vise with the cutting edge up. Using a bastard file or a grinder, sharpen from the outer edge toward the center. Follow the existing bevel, or, if that's gone, sharpen at a 30-degree angle. Push the file down and across the

length of the cutting edge in one motion, lifting the file on the return. Then repeat.

Don't try to file away deep nicks. Instead, round them out with a small, round file. A V-shaped nick can be the start of a crack. If the blade has any cracks, discard it and buy a replacement. As you sharpen, check periodically to see that the blade remains balanced.

6. After sharpening, check the blade for balance. The best way is to drill a hole through the exact center of a cork and put it in the blade hole. Put a slim screwdriver through the cork hole and hold it horizontally to see if the blade stays level or if one side is heavier and falls. You can also balance the blade by putting it on a nail driven in the shop wall, but the nail must be centered carefully in the hole or else you won't get an accurate balance. If one side is heavier than the other, remove more metal from that side during sharpening.

Engine Maintenance

On all power mowers, good engine maintenance is the key to long life. Change the oil every 25 operating hours to reduce undue engine wear. Always clean the air filter at the same time (more often if the machine operates in dusty conditions). Refer to your owner's manual for detailed instructions, and see pages 77–95 of this book on engine maintenance and tune-ups.

Sharpening a Rotary Mower Blade

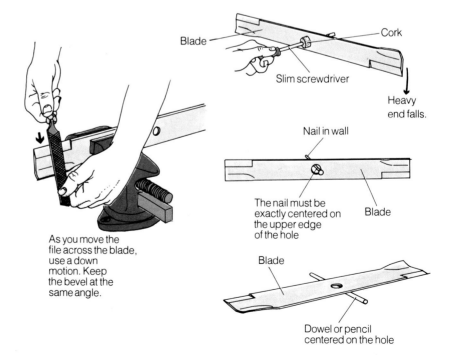

As you move the file across the blade, use a down motion. Keep the bevel at the same angle.

Balancing the Blade

Blade — Cork

Slim screwdriver

Heavy end falls.

Nail in wall

The nail must be exactly centered on the upper edge of the hole

Blade

Blade

Dowel or pencil centered on the hole

RIDING MOWERS AND SMALL TRACTORS

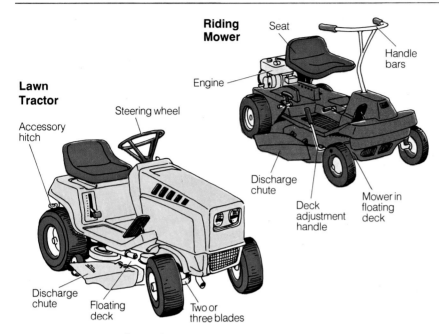

Lawn Tractor
- Accessory hitch
- Steering wheel
- Discharge chute
- Floating deck
- Two or three blades

Riding Mower
- Seat
- Handle bars
- Engine
- Discharge chute
- Deck adjustment handle
- Mower in floating deck

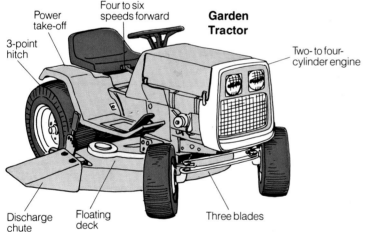

Garden Tractor
- Power take-off
- Four to six speeds forward
- 3-point hitch
- Two- to four-cylinder engine
- Discharge chute
- Floating deck
- Three blades

If your lawn is very large, consider a riding mower, a lawn tractor, or (for really big jobs) a garden tractor.

The *riding mower* lets you do just what the name implies. Most major brands of riding mowers have such options as mower-mulcher attachments and grass collectors to ease your clean-up chores. These models range from 6 to 10 horsepower and include both battery engines and gasoline-powered engines with battery, rope, or rewind starters.

The *lawn tractor* is a larger version of the riding mower. Its horsepower ranges from 8 to 12. Between one and three rotary cutting blades will handle swaths up to 42 inches wide. If you are considering buying one of these models, read the fine print: You may find that the price does not include the mowing attachment (the mowing deck), which is just one of several attachments available.

The *garden tractor* has 5 to 30-horsepower engines that are fueled by either gasoline or diesel. (See page 85 for a discussion of the relative merits of diesel and gasoline engines.) Several manufacturers offer four-wheel-drive vehicles for greater pulling power. The wide variety of farming implements available make this tractor ideal for the spare-time farmer.

Whether you are planning to buy a riding lawn mower, a lawn tractor, or a garden tractor, keep this rule in mind: It is better to buy equipment that is slightly *more* (rather than less) powerful than you need. Whatever type you buy, you will almost certainly use it more than anticipated.

Attachments

Many attachments are available for riding mowers, lawn tractors, and garden tractors, including the following: mowing decks, grass collectors, utility carts, lawn sweepers, spreader seeders, harrows, and snowblowers. Most tractors also have lawn aerators, front-mounted snow/dozer blades, plows, and discs. Examine the selection available, and find out if the hitch on your model will take implements made by other manufacturers.

Basic Safety Rules

Riding mowers and tractors may look like big toys, but they can be dangerous in the hands of careless or unskilled operators. To avoid accidents, follow these suggestions:

☐ When using a mower, first check the area to be cut—is there any debris that might be thrown across the lawn by the rotary blade? If so, remove it.

☐ Do not allow any passengers, particularly small children, to ride with you. A bump could throw them off.

☐ On hills, always mow up and down the slope rather than across it. This will prevent the machine from tipping over on its side.

☐ If your tractor has a key, always remove it when the machine is parked. Not only does this reduce the chance of theft but it also prevents children from starting the machine. Park tractors in neutral; make sure the power takeoff is disengaged and the safety brake is set.

☐ Before letting anyone (especially children) operate the machinery, teach them how to handle it.

Maintenance

Cleaning
After each use, hose down your riding mower or tractor to remove damp dirt. Then wipe it dry or let it sun-dry.

Sharpening
After every third use of your rotary mower, remove and sharpen the blades. Follow instructions in the owner's manual to remove the mowing deck. Then use the procedure outlined on the facing page to sharpen the blades.

Lubrication
Because heavier demands are made on lawn and garden tractors, they have several grease fittings on such places as the wheels, steering gears, and drive shaft. (See your owner's manual for the specific locations.) These tractors need to be greased annually, twice annually if used regularly. A grease gun with a flexible hose to reach in narrow areas is a necessity.

Engine Maintenance
For these machines (as well as all other kinds of power equipment), become well acquainted with your owner's manual and see pages 77–95 of this book.

TRIMMERS AND EDGERS

Trimming means cutting horizontally. It usually is done around trees, fences, and other obstructions to prevent a ridge of long grass from growing up around them. Edging means cutting vertically. It keeps the edges of the lawn next to walks and garden beds looking crisp and neat.

Traditionally, these jobs have been done with grass shears, the wheeled multi-toothed rotary edger, or the semicircular turf edger. In recent years, however, electric and gas-powered tools have become more popular. Although some tools are designed to do only one job, many can be used for either trimming or edging.

Which type of tool you choose depends largely on the size of the job, how fast you want to accomplish it, and whether you want to invest in the more expensive power tools. If you want to "trench" the edge, you'll need equipment with digging capacity.

Types of Trimmers and Edgers

Grass Shears
Sitting on the grass and trimming with hand shears may be laborious, but it affords a certain satisfaction. There are two basic types of hand shears: (1) the tradi-tional sheep-shearer design, in which the shears are simply squeezed together, and (2) spring-activated shears, with vinyl-covered handles and a vertical squeeze. The latter is more comfortable for extensive trimming. In both types, the blades must be kept sharp to be efficient.

Battery-Operated Shears
Battery-operated shears are a boon for those who like to trim by hand but just don't have the strength. All you need to do is point these shears in the right direction and turn on the switch. They will cut for 30 to 40 minutes at a time and fully recharge in 24 hours. However, they are good only for trimming grass and very light weeds. Heavy material will cause the engine to strain and "lug down," possibly burning out the tiny motor. Shears often have re-placeable blades. They cost only a couple of dollars and can be replaced each year, which saves you the bother of sharpening blades.

Semicircular Turf Edger
This tool looks like a hoe that has been straightened out and trimmed to a half-moon shape. With its curved edge that is beveled on one side and kept sharp like a hoe, the tool will cut through soil as well as grass. It is used primarily for cutting the lawn next to a sidewalk and straightening up crooked edges. It doesn't work for reg-ular trimming, however, because it takes off a little soil each time. Therefore don't use it too often or your lawn will get smaller and smaller. Once or twice a year will do for trimming. You can also use it to cut out sections of turf. Its construction is very similar to that of a hoe (see page 31).

Rotary Edger
When the wheels roll along the surface next to the lawn, the rolling action drives the multitoothed rotary blades. These blades cut and trench flush with the outer edge of the flower bed, sidewalk, or drive-way. Models come with either one wide wheel or two wheels (the latter provide more control and balance).

On some models, the rotary blade can be adjusted to two or three different cutting depths. Before you buy this feature, con-sider whether you really need it.

Electric Edger
The electric cord limits the reach of these ½ to 1-horsepower edgers, but many homeowners like the instant power and quiet, largely maintenance-free motor. With extension cords, these edgers can work from 50 to 100 feet from a power source.

Hand Trimmers and Edgers

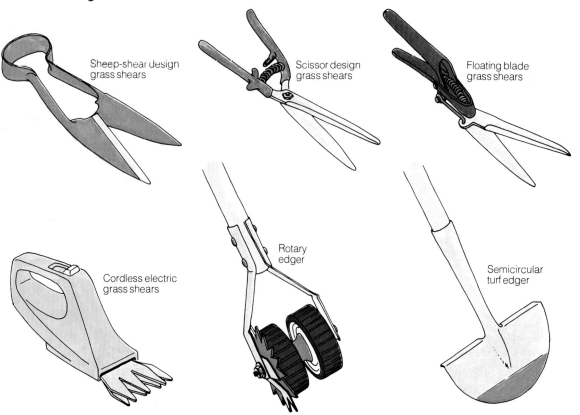

Sheep-shear design grass shears

Scissor design grass shears

Floating blade grass shears

Cordless electric grass shears

Rotary edger

Semicircular turf edger

Power Trimmers and Edgers

Combination Edger and trimmer

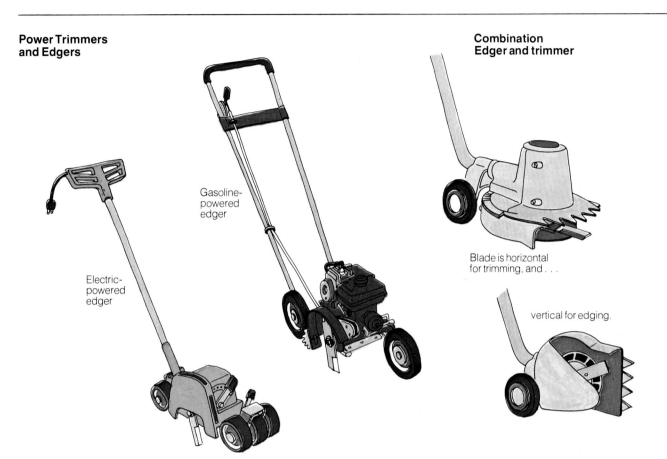

Electric-powered edger

Gasoline-powered edger

Blade is horizontal for trimming, and . . .

vertical for edging.

The diameter of the edging blade ranges from 6 to 8 inches and leaves a trench varying from 0 to 2 inches deep. If depth adjustment is available, it normally is made with a lever on the handle. The power button is built into the top of the handle. As a safety feature, on some models this button cannot be locked in the "on" position; the power is cut immediately when the switch is released. On other types, an automatic blade-brake stops the blade within seconds after the power is cut. Because the power edgers can send rocks or chips of concrete flying, goggles or other eye protectors are highly recommended.

Gas-Powered Edgers

Gasoline-powered edgers come in a wide variety of engine sizes. Which to choose depends on how much edging you must regularly do. The four-cycle engines range from 2 to 4 horsepower.

Most models have two wheels at the rear for stability, and another in the front for guidance and ease in maneuvering over curbs.

Since they are more powerful than electric models, they can support blade lengths up to 10 inches to make cuts from 0 to 4 inches deep. Depth adjustments are made by a lever on the handlebars.

Some models convert into trimmers when a lever that tilts the blade from vertical to horizontal is pulled. Some models offer nine different blade angles within a range of 120 degrees. The trimming width matches the overall blade length. The edger has a blade guard that prevents debris from being tossed toward the operator; when the edger is used as a trimmer, the blade guard keeps the blade from striking walls or tree trunks. Despite this safety device, however, goggles or other eye protectors are recommended.

Maintenance

Cleaning
All edgers, whether hand-operated or powered, should be kept clean, rust-free, and lightly oiled.

Sharpening
Grass shears. Because shears, like scissors, are somewhat self-sharpening, they don't need to be sharpened too often. If you do want to touch them up, however, use a smooth file or a whetstone and carefully follow the existing bevel on the outside of the blade. Never touch the inside edge where the blades cross each other or you will create a small gap that ruins the effectiveness of the cutting.

If the shears are already fairly sharp, hone them on a bench stone. Set the edge of the shears on the stone at the correct bevel angle and pull the blade toward you, as if you were trying to slice off a thin layer of the stone.

Battery-operated shears. These reciprocating-action blades are not normally sharpened. Just replace the blade.

Rotary edger. With most models, two steel honing blades built into the housing lightly grind each tooth on the rotary blade as the blade passes. Thus it is self-sharpening. If you find it increasingly difficult to make the edger do the job right, touch up each tooth with a file every month or two.

Semicircular turf edger. Sharpen this tool just like a hoe. Place it in a vise and follow the bevel with a mill file in one long motion (see page 32).

Electric and gas-powered edgers. When the edger blades become dull, remove and sharpen them. Use a bastard file and follow the existing bevel. If the bevel is worn away, file the new edge at about 75 degrees in order to keep a lot of metal behind the edge. To maintain and tune edgers with gasoline or electric engines, see pages 77–95.

NYLON STRING TRIMMERS AND BRUSH CUTTERS

The nylon string trimmer ranks with the lawn mower and rotary tiller as a major time-saving gardening tool: A grass- or weed-trimming job that takes half a day by hand can be done in half an hour or less with this power tool. While it was designed for trimming, it can also be tilted for edging along walks or garden beds.

The trimmer cuts by the rapid whirling action of a motor-driven nylon string. This method has a great advantage over such hand tools as grass whips or sickles: You can cut right against walls. When the flexible nylon filament strikes an obstruction, it does not break but merely wears away. When this happens, more nylon can be fed out.

These versatile, lightweight tools are run by battery, electricity, or gas-powered engines. A nylon string trimming attachment is also available for some small chainsaws.

Gas-powered brush cutters do regular trimming and also provide you with the option of replacing the nylon spool with blades for cutting light brush or tree limbs. Unless you have a lot of brush to cut, you probably won't need this version.

Selection. Which type and size to choose depends on what you'll need to do with it. If you have a large lawn or garden that demands a variety of cutting chores, start out by renting or borrowing a trimmer. If it won't easily handle your toughest weeds, you need a more powerful model.

Power is determined by the size of the electric motor or the two-cycle gasoline engine. Electric models range from ⅛ to about ¾ horsepower. Gas-operated models are rated by the size of the engine in cubic centimeters (cc). A 20 to 25-cc engine will handle most heavy trimming or brush cutting work, even on a large estate, but to be sure that this fits your needs, rent one and try it out.

The width of the cutting swath is directly related to the power of the engine. The swath ranges from about 7 inches for the battery-operated or small electric trimmers up to about 20 inches for the large, gas-powered types. Any attempt to increase the nylon whip length beyond its rating will unnecessarily strain the engine.

Feed system. Select a model that has an automatic or semiautomatic feed system for the nylon whip. Trimmers with these systems contain a spool of nylon filament in the cutting head. Lengths are fed out in either of two ways: (1) automatically, by a sensor in the cutting head that automatically keeps the nylon at a certain length or (2) semiautomatically, by your rapping the base of the cutting head on the ground to release about 1 inch of nylon whip at a time. A knife edge in the rear guard trims off the frayed end and prevents too much cord from being put out. Some other models require you to stop the engine and replace the whip by hand each time it wears down. This is time-consuming and frustrating when you are working in dense weeds that quickly wear away the nylon.

Nylon. Spools containing up to 50 feet of nylon can be bought from trimmer dealers. On some models, two to four whips extend from the spool, offering greater cutting capacity. The nylon comes in different gauges, ranging from the small .051 up to the heavy 130. The smaller the motor or engine, the smaller filament you must use.

Design. On the most popular models, the motor or gas engine is at the top of the handle and a long drive shaft inside the handle is attached to the cutting head. On others, the engine is mounted directly on the cutting head, which eliminates the problems that may come with a long drive shaft; however, because the engine is closer to the ground, the air filter may get clogged with dust or debris.

The handles (and, in the case of those with top-mounted engines, the drive shaft) are either straight or flexed (curved). A straight drive shaft has a more efficient design; therefore it normally is used on heavy-duty trimmers and on the majority of brush cutters.

For your own comfort, a trimmer should be balanced, particularly if you might use it for two or three hours at a time. Before buying, check the balance by holding each model as if you were using it. A few models have handles that can be adjusted in length according to your height.

If you choose a brush cutter, be sure the blades can be easily interchanged. At least two different blades should be available, one with 4 to 8 teeth for whacking off light brush and heavy weeds and another with 40 to 80 teeth for cutting small brush and limbs.

Safety

Always wear sturdy shoes or boots when using a string trimmer or brush cutter. Also wear goggles—a brush cutter tends to throw materials as it cuts.

Using the Nylon String Trimmer

Walk along the wall, tree, or fence holding the trimmer close to the ground. The nylon filament cuts the grass in record time.

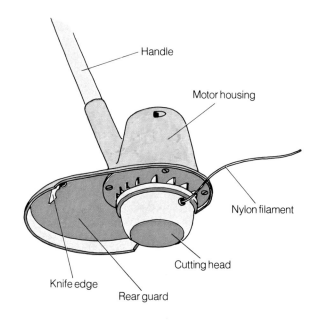

Handle

Motor housing

Nylon filament

Cutting head

Rear guard

Knife edge

Trimmers and Brush Cutters

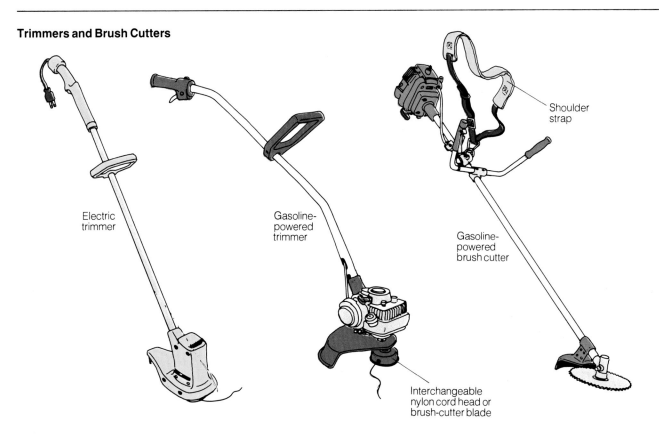

Electric trimmer

Gasoline-powered trimmer

Gasoline-powered brush cutter

Shoulder strap

Interchangeable nylon cord head or brush-cutter blade

Types of Trimmers and Brush Cutters

Battery-Operated Trimmers
These, the smallest of the trimmers, are handy for light trimming and edging around a small yard. The battery, which provides power for about 45 minutes of trimming, will recharge when plugged into a standard 110-outlet over a 24-hour period. The cutting swath on battery trimmers is usually about 6 to 8 inches wide. Usually, the nylon string is advanced semiautomatically by tapping the base on the ground. There are also models with manual advance.

Electric Trimmers
These least-expensive trimmers will handle small to medium trimming work within 50 to 100 feet of an outlet. They are lightweight and quiet, with cutting swaths that range from about 7 to 18 inches wide. Models come with both automatic and semiautomatic nylon line feed.

The horsepower on electric trimmers usually ranges from 1/8 to 3/4. When operating an electric trimmer, do not let the motor strain and "lug down" during heavy cutting, or it will overheat and possibly burn out. Keep the motor running at high revolution, and move slowly in dense weeds or grass.

Some models have a switch to reduce the power consumption when doing light trim work. This power reduction also helps extend the life of the motor.

Gasoline-Powered Trimmers
If your trimming chores are more extensive than you can handle comfortably with a battery or electric-powered machine, the gas-powered trimmer is for you. There are many options available in the cutting swath, the nylon cord feed system, and in the engine size, which ranges from 14 cubic centimeters to 30 cubic centimeters. Choose according to the size of the job and your own convenience. The main disadvantage of this trimmer is that its gas engine needs more maintenance. It is also quite a bit heavier than the other types. Even if you are very strong, you'll probably have to rest after 20 or 30 minutes.

Gasoline-Powered Brush Cutters
The brush cutter can do all that a gas-powered trimmer can, plus accept steel blades for chopping brush and tree limbs. Brush cutters have heavier drive shafts to accommodate the steel blades. Both the brush cutter and the trimmer are powered by two-cycle engines ranging in size from about 14cc to more than 30cc for the largest professional models. The largest ones have the engine set in a backpack on antivibration mountings.

Brush cutters are significantly more expensive than gas-powered trimmers. Be sure you have enough brush to warrant the additional investment.

Maintenance

Cleaning
Like all garden equipment, wipe and dry these tools before storing them.

Sharpening
Some brush cutters now being made have plastic blades that can be thrown away and replaced when worn. The metal blades can be sharpened with a second file.

Engine Maintenance
Motors for battery and electric trimmers are basically maintenance free (see page 78). Maintain and tune the engines of gas-powered trimmers as detailed on pages 79–95. Many of the newer trimmers have solid-state electronic ignition systems that do away with the need for periodically changing the points and condenser.

On gas-powered models, the air filters should be checked and cleaned regularly, particularly if the engine is mounted on the cutting head, where it receives much dust and debris. A clogged air filter not only reduces the engine's performance but will soon cause engine damage. The shaft of the trimmer is usually a flex wire rope type shaft and should be oiled regularly.

SPREADERS

Hand-Held Broadcast Spreaders

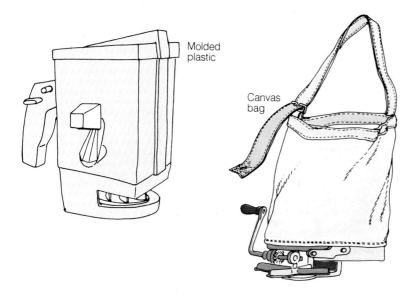

Molded plastic

Canvas bag

Spreaders can do more than just apply fertilizer—they can spread seeds, granular pesticides, ice melters, mulch, gypsum, and more. There are two basic types of spreaders: broadcast and drop.

Broadcast. The broadcast spreader drops fertilizer or other material from a hopper onto a pan that rotates at high speed. The material is flung by centrifugal force in a feather-edge pattern that ranges from a few inches wide to 10 feet or more. This means that there is less material at the edges than in the middle, so overlap is required to give an even distribution. Broadcast spreaders are either hand-held and powered by a crank that you turn as you walk along or pushed or towed and powered by the turning wheels.

Drop. The drop spreader puts down an even layer of material that's about the width of the spreader (from 14 to 30 inches or more). As the material falls from holes in the hopper, it is spread evenly by finned agitators that are linked to the axle. Because the pattern is even, there should be no overlap or else those areas will have too much material. Drop spreaders can be either pushed or towed. No hand-held models are available.

Drop spreaders give much more precise coverage than do broadcast spreaders. This allows you to: Spread fertilizer or pesticides right up to the edge of the lawn without getting any on adjacent flower beds; control the amount of overlap; and avoid blank spots. On the other hand, drop spreaders have a fairly narrow pattern, requiring more passes back and forth across a lawn, and they do not work well on surfaces that aren't level.

Broadcast spreaders are much quicker, more suited to large areas, and very effective on any kind of surface you can walk across. They can be used to spread fertilizer or pesticides across rough ground covers, across the tops of shrubs, or on vegetable gardens. However, because they lack the precision of placement and coverage offered by the drop spreader, drop spreaders are preferred for lawns.

Choose a spreader in terms of its capacity to do your biggest job. Before buying the material to be spread, consult the instructions that come with the spreader to find out the number of pounds you need per acre and what setting to use for the feed-slot opening.

Types of Spreaders

Hand-Held Broadcast Spreaders

The all-plastic type of broadcast spreader is hand-held by a pistol grip, holds about 2 pounds of material, and broadcasts from 4 to 12 feet. Excellent for small to medium-size lawns, these are the ones most commonly used by homeowners.

Another type has a canvas-bag hopper with a wood base and a plastic spreading-platform. This spreader will hold about 10 pounds and spread material in a 4 to 16-foot-wide pattern. Because this type holds so much more material, it is quite heavy; consequently it is used more by professionals than by homeowners.

Wheeled Broadcast Spreaders

These large, wheeled spreaders, which

Push Spreaders

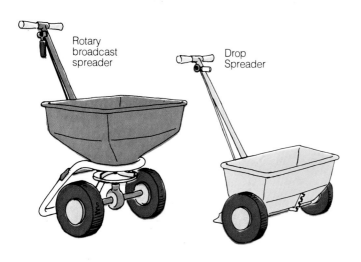

Rotary broadcast spreader

Drop Spreader

Drop Spreader Pattern

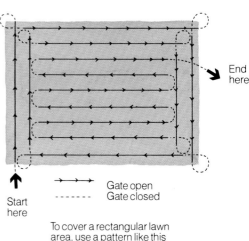

End here

Start here

→ → → Gate open
- - - - Gate closed

To cover a rectangular lawn area, use a pattern like this (see text on next page).

LAWN SWEEPERS

work on the same principle as the hand-held model, are designed to cover a wide area quickly and are most effective on flat, large lawns. They are commonly made of plastic or of steel with a baked epoxy or enamel finish to counter the corrosive qualities of fertilizers and pesticides. The hoppers are square or round, and their capacities range from 20 to 80 pounds for push models, up to more than 100 pounds for tractor-pulled types. On most models the spreading pattern can be adjusted from about 4 to 10 feet in a half circle. The feed opening is set by a lever on the handlebars.

Drop Spreaders
These spreaders cover an area only about the width of the hopper (from 14 to 30 inches in the push models, wider in tractor-pulled models). Its limited spreading width makes it slower than the broadcast spreader, but it gives a more uniform distribution. It is a good choice for seeding lawns because of this precise pattern.

The hopper holds 30 to 80 pounds of material, depending on the model. Some models are made to work only with fertilizers, seeds, or pesticides made by the spreader manufacturer. Most models have a calibrated metering device, controlled by a lever on the handlebars, that is set according to instructions for the material to be spread.

Spreaders are designed in such a way that they drop material when you turn in one direction but not in the other. Since this makes it slightly difficult to apply material evenly, follow the pattern illustrated here. Making two passes at each end of the area allows you to close the gate of the spreader as you make each turn and ensures even application (material is being dropped only when you walk at a steady rate in a straight line). Overlap the wheel tracks; this enables the material of one pass, which drops right up to the inside edge of the wheels, to exactly meet the edge of the material dropped on the last pass. As with broadcast spreaders, don't open the gate until you're already walking or you'll drop too much material at the beginning.

Maintenance
Keep hoppers on all spreaders clean and dry so that material will not stick to them. Hose out drop spreaders after each use and let them dry. Do not store them with fertilizers inside—many fertilizers absorb water when exposed to air, and they will cake up into a cementlike substance that's hard to get rid of. It's very important to apply a little penetrating oil to the moving parts to keep them from sticking or rusting.

If you have a medium to large-size yard dotted with deciduous trees, a lawn sweeper will make your life easier during fall clean-up (even more of the year if your sweeper will also pick up grass clippings).

Essentially, a sweeper is a set of four to six rows of brushes attached to the axle. The brushes catch the leaves and throw them into the rear collecting bag.

Sweepers usually are pushed, but several models can be towed behind a lawn tractor or riding mower.

To make the best use of a sweeper, your lawn should be smooth and level. Sweepers operate close to the ground, so any irregularities in your lawn can cause problems. Where the ground begins to rise, the sweeper's front end may dig into it; in a depression, the brushes will skip leaves.

In selecting a sweeper, examine its construction. Is it built well enough to hold up under several years of strain?

On push models, most of the force is directed against the handlebars. These, ideally, should be connected directly to the wheels, not to a separate support system that could buckle while going up hills or over rough ground.

Also consider the rear bagger. It should be made of light canvas or heavy nylon to resist tearing and sagging. Plastic bags that tear easily will just cause you grief.

The floor of the bag on a top-quality sweeper is made from galvanized steel or rigid fiberglass. Thus it is rustproof and it is sturdy enough to carry the load of leaves. Most of these good models have a small set of wheels or rollers to support the rear bag. Flooring made of just the bag material or soft vinyl tends to drag on the ground as the bag fills. This friction causes wear and increases your work.

The height of the brushes should be adjustable from 0 to 3 inches in five to eight settings. This is standard and enables you to adapt to different types of leaves and conditions. If you are picking up large, dry oak leaves, you might want a higher setting; however, small, damp leaves, such as willow, need a setting near the ground.

Types of Sweepers

Standard Push Sweeper
This type of sweeper holds between five and seven bushels of leaves. The width usually ranges from 20 to 30 inches. If your lawn is less than perfectly smooth, choose a narrower model—it will fit better into any depressions, whereas the wheels on wider models may span the entire depression and not pick up the leaves.

Towed Lawn Sweepers
These models can be pulled by riding mowers or lawn tractors. In general they are identical to the push models, except that they are wider (they range from 25 to 35 inches) and have a larger capacity (usually seven to nine bushels). This larger capacity means that you need a good collection bag and floor. The tow bar usually is sold separately.

Some towed models have the bag in front of the sweeping brushes. This bag, supported by a frame connected to the tractor, eliminates the need to have small wheels in back. The leaves are picked up by two sets of brushes that throw them forward.

Maintenance
As with all garden equipment, keep the sweeper clean and dry when it isn't in use. Wipe the steel frame with an oily rag to prevent rust. Because the wheel bearings tend to be made of nylon and to be enclosed, no oiling is necessary.

Wash and brush the bag to remove fine material. Clean nylon bags with high-pressure water spray; direct it from the outside of the bag to the inside. Then let the bag dry completely.

Push-Type Lawn Sweeper

PRUNING AND CHAINSAWS

Learn how to select the best pruning tools, how to use them properly, and how to care for them. For big jobs or for cutting wood, a chainsaw is indispensable. This chapter shows you how to use it safely and how to sharpen and maintain it.

Pruning tools come in various styles and shapes. Each one is designed to perform a specific type of pruning, usually on the basis of the size of the branch to be cut.

While it may be obvious that a delicate bonsai should not be pruned with a pair of ratchet loppers, a surprising number of people try to do the reverse and tackle an inch-thick limb with a pair of small hand-pruners. As a result, the pruning blades are sprung and the limb looks like it has been gnawed off. The tree suffers most of all—a poorly cut branch takes longer to heal and is more susceptible to disease. Using the right tool for the job will make all your pruning easier and cleaner.

Selecting Pruning Tools

One of the most important pruning tools costs you nothing: Your thumb and fore-finger. No tool is handier for pinching off tiny buds or leaf tips.

When buying pruners, first consider the cutting blades. They should be top-quality steel, preferably stainless or forged. These will be more durable and will hold their edge.

Forging involves hammering and compressing steel, which makes it more dense and uniform. In this process, the grain of the steel is aligned in the proper direction to provide more strength. Forging also places more steel where it is needed and less where it is not, thereby reinforcing its structure.

Many people are now cutting their own wood. Chainsaws simplify the job.

An alternative approach is to cast or stamp the parts. This is commonly done with cheap to medium-quality tools. Because this process is cheaper, the tool costs less, but the lower-grade metal used won't hold up as long.

Pick up any tool you are considering buying and inspect it closely. If you see rough edges on the finish, you can be sure that it was cast or stamped. Check that the blades come together smoothly and that the blades touch each other along their entire length when you close them. Look for any loose parts or poor workmanship. If the tool fails to pass this basic inspection, don't even bother with it—it will turn pruning from an enjoyable hobby into an unpleasant chore.

Using shears properly . . .

A hand pruner is designed to cut live wood up to ¾ inch thick.

. . . and improperly

Using hand pruners on wood that is too dry or too thick can damage the pruner. If you can't make the cut easily with one hand, use a lopper or saw.

You can also purchase Teflon-coated blades, which are designed to pass through wood more smoothly; however, not all gardeners and pruners can notice the difference. Since normal use may eventually wear off the coating, a comparable tool without Teflon may serve you just as well.

Handles also are important. Since they vary in style, materials, and construction according to the type of tool, consult the following sections for specific advice.

Finally, ask the dealer if the broken or worn parts can be replaced. This will save you the expense of buying a new tool. Some manufacturers offer repair kits that include nuts, bolts, blades, anvils, and springs.

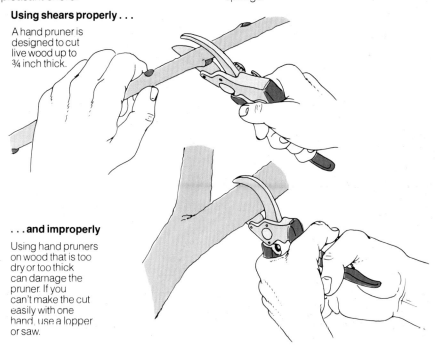

HAND PRUNERS (SECATEURS)

Bypass Blade Pruner

Anvil Blade Pruner

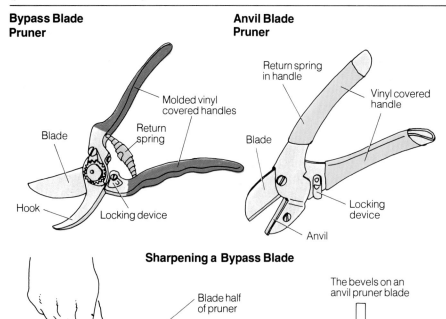

Molded vinyl covered handles

Return spring

Blade

Hook

Locking device

Return spring in handle

Vinyl covered handle

Blade

Locking device

Anvil

Sharpening a Bypass Blade

Blade half of pruner

Vise

Move whetstone down and toward the tip of the blade

The bevels on an anvil pruner blade

Blade

45°   85°

Anvil

The most ubiquitous pruning tool in the country is probably the hand pruner, or secateur. These range from small floral shears (used to cut flowers) to large hand shears that can cut ¾-inch-diameter branches. Because such a wide variety is available, you may have a hard time deciding which to buy.

Basically, there are two styles of hand pruners: (1) those with a bypass blade and (2) those with an anvil blade. The bypass blade is generally superior in that you can get it close to the trunk for a clean cut. Also, it is not as apt to crush the end of a twig as the anvil blade.

In both types, the handles are covered with molded vinyl for comfort and gripping ease. A return spring opens the blade after each cut. Most hand pruners have a locking device to keep them closed for carrying or storage. Those with locking devices at the rear of the handle may cause blisters on the heel of your palm.

Since the size of the grips can vary considerably, spend a few minutes trying out several to see which feels most comfortable. Choose carefully: Pruning for 30 minutes to an hour or two is tiring. You may want handles that do not spring open wider than the size of your hand.

Types of Secateurs

Bypass Hand Pruner

This uses a scissor-action bypass style. Because the cutting blade usually is tapered and thin, these tools are effective in narrow spots among limbs. The blade passes against the "hook" or lower blade that is curved to catch and hold the branch while the cutting blade comes down on it. Bypass pruners give a smooth and accurate cut close to the tree. Good bypass pruners are made of stainless steel or forged steel. The overall length of most of these pruners is about 7 to 9 inches. On good types, the parts are replaceable.

Anvil Hand Pruners

Here, the cutting blade comes down in the center of a soft metal or hard plastic anvil. The design of these pruners allows them to cut larger branches with less probability that the blades will be sprung. But because the blade comes down in the anvil, you cannot cut as close to the trunk as with bypass secateurs, and you are more likely to leave a small stub. When you're cutting through a branch, angle the pruning blades so that you are not cutting directly across the grain of the wood but rather at a diagonal. This will offer less resistance.

Unlike bypass pruners, anvil hand pruners are not made from forged steel, even when of top quality. Forging is not considered necessary because of the direct cutting action and the soft metal required in the anvil. But look for tools that have specially hardened and tempered cutting edges.

Maintenance

Cleaning

Keeping the shears clean is vital to their effectiveness. Disease can be spread from plant to plant, and sap can gum up the action (even though many secateurs have sap grooves in the hook to carry the sap away). During extensive pruning, carry a rag in your pocket to wipe sticky blades down, or use a jackknife to scrape the blades whenever they start sticking. Always clean away any debris that gets caught between the blades or else the blades won't close properly.

Sharpening

To take secateurs apart for cleaning or sharpening, follow the direction indicated by the small arrows on the bolt head (some are reverse-threaded). If the secateurs can't be taken apart, you will have to prop them open.

Remember that clippers and shears are beveled only on the outside of a blade. The inside of these blades, where they meet when closed, should never be filed—this would create a slight gap and inhibit the slicing action. So never try to file off any burrs on the unbeveled side; simply snap them off by closing the blade.

On curved-blade pruning shears, normally only one of the blades is beveled for cutting. The other, the hook, is square-edged and should not be touched up.

To sharpen a blade that has been separated, clamp it in a vise. Use a whetstone and move it down against the edge and around the curve. Work from the area nearest the pivot toward the tip. At the end of each pass, lift the stone and repeat.

For small pruning shears that cannot be taken apart, spread the handles and follow the same procedure as discussed above.

Anvil-type shears often have two beveled edges, the first about 45 degrees and the second, a narrow one right near the edge, at about 85 degrees. (You may have to use a magnifying glass to see it.) Take the shears apart and sharpen only the small bevel next to the edge. This is best done on a bench stone.

Inspect anvils regularly to detect deep grooves; these can impair the cutting ability and ultimately tear the bark. If the blade is too deeply grooved or worn to be sharpened, replace it.

LOPPERS

If you need to cut a limb ¾ inch thick or more, don't risk damaging your hand pruner—reach for the loppers instead. Loppers are the larger version of hand pruners; they will take on any limb up to 2 inches in diameter.

Loppers are usually made in the bypass style, although the anvil style is also available. Use the bypass for finer close-to-the-trunk work; use the anvil type for less precise cutting. A new ratchet-action lopper is also on the market. This is cranked closed, like a car jack. The leverage it offers allows you to cut much larger branches.

Good cutting heads on bypass loppers are made from forged steel. Many are coated with Teflon to reduce blade friction in the wood. Anvil-type loppers are not forged, but the good ones have cutting edges that have been specially hardened and tempered.

A wide variety of handles is available. Straight-grained ash or hickory are the proven standbys. Solid steel handles provide great strength, but they increase the weight. Tubular steel or fiberglass handles are lighter but not as strong. Look for han-dles that have rubber cushions to absorb the shock when the loppers snap shut.

Types of Loppers

Standard Bypass Lopper
This style of lopper has wood handles and a bypass cutting head made from forged steel or a chrome alloy steel for greater rust resistance. This is one of the most important pruning tools you can own.

Lengths range from 12 to 18 inches for medium-size loppers and 24 to 28 inches for larger ones. The longer handles provide more leverage in heavy cutting.

The cutting head on bypass loppers is more pointed than on most anvil types, which enables it to work more easily in narrow spots among limbs.

Because bypass loppers cut closer to the trunk than do anvil pruners, no stub is left. For a smooth cut, place the cutting blade on the underside of the limb.

Anvil Loppers
In addition to the standard hinged action, which works as it does on secateurs, the anvil lopper comes in two modified ver-sions that provide more cutting power.

In the first version, the head contains a small set of gears that (according to manu-facturers' claims) provide up to three times more leverage for easier cutting. Because of the gears, the head is slightly wider than normal; thus, it won't cut a branch flush with the trunk. Use this lopper for general and heavy pruning.

Another type of anvil lopper with in-creased cutting power uses a ratchet ac-tion. The handles must be opened and shut several times to increase the ratch-et-action power, so it takes more time to complete a cut. However, the cutting is easier to do. This is a good choice if you don't feel physically strong enough for the heavier pruning.

Maintenance
Most loppers can be taken apart for con-venient cleaning and sharpening. Clean the blades of any vegetation and wipe them with an oily rag or hose them off and spray with a penetrating oil. Sharpen the cutting head according to the sharpening instructions for bypass and anvil hand pruners (page 50).

Loppers

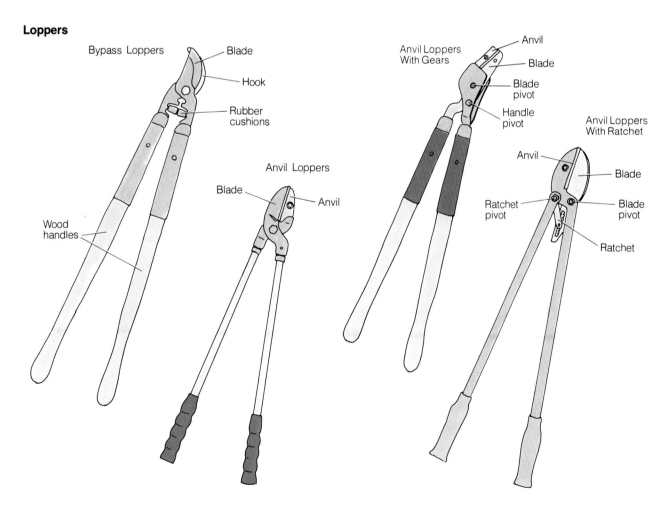

Bypass Loppers — Blade — Hook — Rubber cushions — Wood handles

Anvil Loppers — Blade — Anvil

Anvil Loppers With Gears — Anvil — Blade — Blade pivot — Handle pivot

Anvil Loppers With Ratchet — Anvil — Blade — Ratchet pivot — Blade pivot — Ratchet

PRUNING SAWS

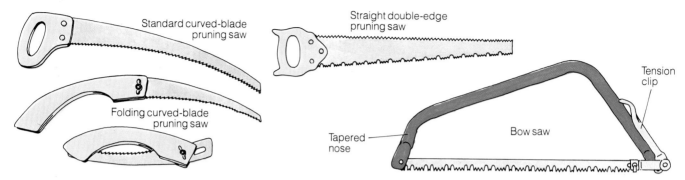

Standard curved-blade pruning saw

Folding curved-blade pruning saw

Straight double-edge pruning saw

Tapered nose

Bow saw

Tension clip

If you plan to do some serious pruning, you'll need a pruning saw—it's the third most important item after hand shears and loppers. Pruning saws come in styles that can handle limbs from 2 to 25 inches in diameter.

Because the teeth on the standard curved pruning saw are angled back, the cutting action is on the pull. This makes it easier to do overhead work—the curve in the blade automatically forces the teeth into the kerf (the cut) as you pull.

The blade should be made of tempered steel. Although tempering may not be marked, if you snap the blade with your fingernail it will emit a clear, ringing sound if it *is* tempered. The blade should be flexible; that way, when it catches and bends in the kerf, it will immediately snap back to its original straight position. When a saw blade gets bent, it must be replaced.

Check the number of teeth per inch. They usually run from four to eight. Four to six teeth per inch is good for green or sap wood; six to eight teeth per inch is a better choice for hard or dry wood. If you have a mixture of woods, consider the double-edged saw with a combination of both teeth.

Look carefully at each individual tooth. On a good saw, each tooth will be beveled to provide the cutting edge. Teeth on cheaper saws have no cutting bevel.

Types of Saw Teeth

Peg teeth on a curved pruning saw

Cutting direction

Tooth and gullet combination

Gullet   Cutter teeth

Raker   Cutter teeth   Gullet

Cutter and raker teeth

Types of Pruning Saws

Standard Curved-Blade Saw
This is the workhorse saw for nursery-people and home pruners. This spring steel blade is 12 to 16 inches long; six teeth per inch do all-purpose cutting.

The handle is made of ash or hickory. It has a comfortable grip for sawing at any angle, including overhead.

Straight Double-Edged Saw
This is a good combination saw for medium and heavy pruning. One side has six or eight teeth per inch with small gullets for cutting hard or dry wood. The other side has four to six larger, raker teeth per inch for quickly cutting green or sap wood.

When using these saws, be careful not to inadvertently gash one limb with the saw's top edge while trying to saw another limb. Wounds like these subject the tree to disease and pests.

Pole Saw
The above saws can also come on the end of a long pole for reaching high or inaccessible branches. See "Pole Pruners" (next page) for a description of handles.

Bow Saw
These saws come in a wide variety of sizes to cut wood anywhere from 10 to 25 inches in diameter. If you plan to use a bow saw for pruning, choose a type with a tapered nose. This enables the front end to slip past other limbs on the tree more easily. A tension clip holds the blades in position. Because of this tension, the metal is much thinner than it is on saws that must support their own rigidity. Therefore, it makes a smaller kerf and cutting goes considerably faster and easier than with an ordinary pruning saw. The bow saw is definitely preferred for cutting large limbs or in uncrowded cutting conditions.

Maintenance
Always remove vegetation from the saw blade and wipe the blade down with an oily rag or spray with a penetrating oil.

Since the teeth on most pruning saws are angled back (they are straight on con-ventional saws), they are difficult to sharpen by machine. This means they must be sharpened by hand. You can pay extra to have this done professionally, or you can do it yourself—probably well enough, too.

First place the saw between two boards in a vise to keep the blade from bending while you work on it. Use a web file or a knife file about 6 to 8 inches long. Note that every tooth on the saw is beveled at an angle opposite the one preceding it.

Sharpening a Pruning Saw

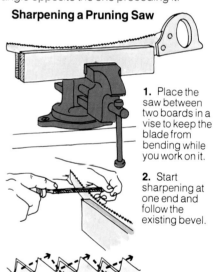

1. Place the saw between two boards in a vise to keep the blade from bending while you work on it.

2. Start sharpening at one end and follow the existing bevel.

3. File the leading bevel of one tooth and the trailing bevel of the next simultaneously. File every other gullet from one side, then reverse the saw and do the rest from the other side.

Cheap saws may have no bevel but be ground straight across like a crosscut saw.

Start sharpening at one end. Follow the existing bevel, which should be about 65 degrees. If there is no bevel, file straight across. Simultaneously file the leading bevel of one tooth and the trailing bevel of the adjoining tooth. Skip every other gullet and file the beveled edges first on one side, then—reversing the saw—on the other side.

File all the teeth evenly, making the same number of strokes at the same pressure in each gullet. Five or six strokes per gullet should be sufficient.

POLE PRUNERS

Recently, the pole pruner has become popular, probably because it largely eliminates the need for a ladder. You may *prefer* a ladder, however—it will keep you from getting a crick in your neck and will let you reach every branch, even those on top.

The pruning head of the pole pruner has a bypass-action blade (which sometimes has a ratchet action) and a pronounced hook. The head works either by a lever and metal rod or by a rope with single or double pulleys. Pruning heads should be made of steel or heavy aluminum alloy. Because pole pruners are subjected to great stress, the cheaper heads will not hold up.

The handle is made of wood, fiberglass, or metal. The fiberglass or metal types are available in handy telescoping models.

The two telescoping fiberglass poles are each 6 feet long. They will adjust to any length between 6 and 11 feet. There are two ways to lock poles into position: (1) by a wing nut or (2) by twisting one pole within the other (this is quick, easy, and very secure).

Metal poles are not recommended where electric lines run through trees, since they present a serious danger.

To use the pole pruner, slip the hook over the branch where you want to make the cut. Put tension on this hook and then make the cut by pulling down the lever or rope. After each cut, use the hook to pull the branch out of the tree to keep the tree clear as you work. You don't want to leave unsightly branches or risk having them fall on someone later. Pulling out the cut branches also makes it easier to see what you've been doing.

Pole Pruners

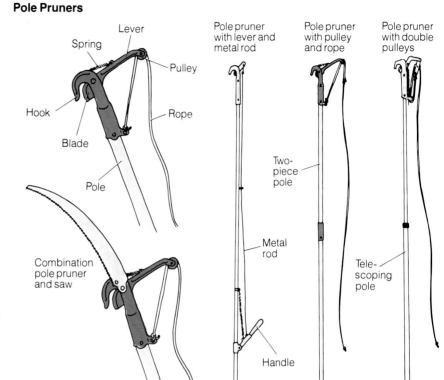

Combination Pruner

You can also buy a pole pruner that has a saw attachment. The 12 to 16-inch saw blade is curved, and the teeth are angled back to make the cutting action occur on the pull stroke rather than on the push stroke. This attachment is used for pruning bigger branches. It can easily be detached when not needed.

Maintenance

Keep the cutting heads and saw blades on all pole pruners clean, sharp, and lightly oiled. For details on sharpening the cutting head, see page 50. The teeth on a saw blade are very long, and the set or spread of the teeth is much greater than on a regular saw. Use a web or slim, tapered, triangular file to sharpen these teeth.

Using a Pole Pruner

1. Put the hook over the branch you want to cut.

2. Pull the rope or lever to cut the branch.

3. Use the hook on the pruner to pull the cut branch from the tree.

HEDGE SHEARS

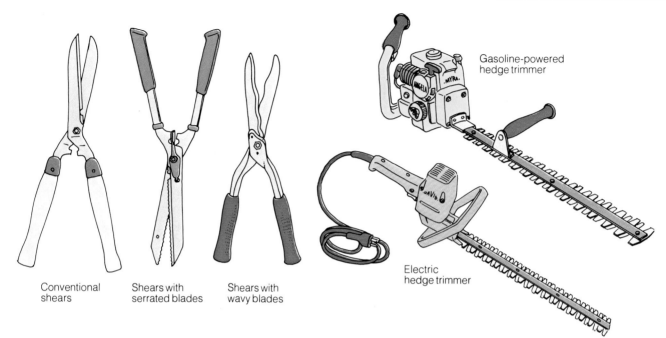

Conventional shears

Shears with serrated blades

Shears with wavy blades

Gasoline-powered hedge trimmer

Electric hedge trimmer

Hedge shears come in hand and powered models. Both are designed to shape bushes and hedges. Normally, power shears will cut only up to ¼-inch-diameter branches; hand shears will trim branches up to ½ inch thick. Some hand shears also have a pruning notch near the pivot point for effectively grabbing and cutting 1-inch limbs. For thicker branches, use lopping shears so you don't risk damaging the hedge shears.

The traditional problem with hand shears was that the heavier branches tended to slip ahead of the blades as they closed. However, two innovations have remedied the situation: (1) one style has wavy blades so that the branch is caught and held in one of the waves and (2) the other style has serrations on one or both blades to catch and hold the branches. If you are planning to buy hedge shears, get those with one of these innovations.

Whether handles are made of wood, steel, or another material, a small but important detail to look for is rubber cushions between the handles. Then, when the blades snap shut, it's these cushions, not your arms, that absorb the shock.

In addition to hand shears, there are also electric and gas-engine hedge shears. These are useful if you have lots of hedges to trim, but they don't equal hand shears for cutting heavy branches. If you have trouble figuring out whether you have enough hedges to justify buying power shears, take the advice of some nursery-people: You do if you have more than 50 feet of hedge.

In selecting hedge shears, look for one with enough power to do the job efficiently.

And consider the blade length. Blades range from 12 to 30 inches, but if you have an average lawn or garden, you don't really need a long blade. It costs more and may unbalance the power hedger. A 16-inch blade is generally adequate.

Types of Shears

Hand Shears
The overall length of these shears generally runs from 12 to 28 inches; the blades are between 6 and 12 inches long. Smaller models are less tiring to use, but they are more time-consuming; longer blades cut level or vertical sides of hedges more accurately.

The best shears are made from stainless steel, but forged steel is nearly as good and markedly cheaper.

When selecting shears, check that the blades come smoothly together along their entire length as they close. If they don't, they will not cut properly. It takes some skill, or at least a lot of care, to use them properly, but it's worth it—hand shears let you prune your hedges more selectively.

Power Shears
Both shears powered by electricity and those powered by a small two-cycle engine work on the same principle: A reciprocating cutting blade runs back and forth beneath a stationary blade. Both blades are notched to catch and hold the small branches as they are cut. Some models have two notched cutting blades and the stationary blade. Most are designed to handle up to ¼-inch-thick branches.

Electric models are convenient, but you

are limited by the length of the power cord. On smaller models, this cord may be no longer than 25 feet long. The longer the cord, the more resistance, which diminishes the electrical power. The cord has a tendency to get in the way, and you must take extra care not to slice it in two while you are pruning.

Gas-powered models are run by small, efficient, two-cycle engines and allow you unencumbered movement. These engines have carburetors designed to work in all positions. Most of them have a centrifugal clutch, which means that the blades do not start working until the engine speed is increased enough to engage the clutch.

The cutting blades are generally from 12 to 30 inches long (an average user needs only 16 to 20 inches). Blades are treated with a dry lubricant such as graphite powder rather than oil to prevent plant material from sticking to them.

Maintenance
Do not sharpen blades for power hedge shears. When they become worn, replace them.

Before putting away pruning equipment, remove any tree bark, leaves, or other debris that is caught in it. Pay particular attention to hand pruners, loppers, and hedge shears. Debris caught between the blades not only impairs the cutting action but will, if left there, invite rust.

While you are cleaning the tools, check for any loose nuts or screws, and tighten them if necessary.

Finally, wipe all metal parts with an oily rag to prevent rust.

GRAFTING KNIVES

Large curved blade

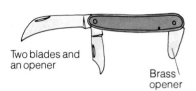

Small straight blade

Two blades and an opener

Brass opener

Grafting is considered an art, and in this case the artist's tools are knives. Grafting knives have straight or curved blades and are thick or thin, depending on the work to be performed.

If you are involved in budding, use a small, straight, thin blade for accuracy. When scion grafting or wedge grafting, use a larger curved blade to cut through hard wood.

Knife blades can be fixed or folding. For convenience, choose a folding knife with two different blades.

A good combination grafting knife has two cutting blades, plus a stubby, dull, brass blade. The larger, heavier cutting blade is for slitting bark, and the dull blade is for opening and spreading the bark before inserting the scion graft into the stock.

Maintenance
For precise grafting, keep the blades clean and extremely sharp by using a fine whetstone.

LADDERS

When picking fruit from a tree, most home-owners use whatever ladder they happen to own. The ladder may be a small to medium-size stepladder, or it may be an extension ladder. While these may get the job done, they are not as safe or as easy to use as the harvest or orchard ladder.

Types of Ladders

Harvest Ladder
The harvest ladder is 8 to 16 feet tall and designed for use among tree limbs. The top is narrow so that it will fit through the

Types of Ladders

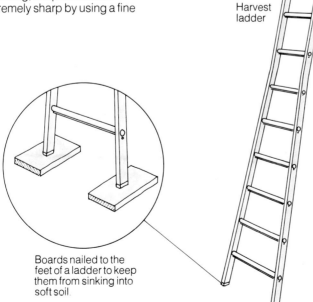

Orchard ladder

Harvest ladder

Boards nailed to the feet of a ladder to keep them from sinking into soft soil.

tangle of branches, and the base is wide to give solid support. Because the narrower top uses less wood in the upper rungs, it is somewhat lighter than a comparable-size untapered ladder. It usually is of a light but strong hardwood, such as ash or basswood.

Orchard Ladder
The orchard ladder (three-legged ladder) differs from the harvest ladder in that it has a center leg that swings out from the top, which makes it free-standing. The leg can be folded back against the rungs when the ladder is carried or leaned against the tree limbs.

The top is narrow to fit past the branches. The base is extra wide to provide support when the ladder is placed in the tripod position.

Safety
Keeping safe on a ladder basically means making sure that it is sturdily braced before you climb it. Extend the ladder fully, and make sure the legs are well planted on the ground, with all the feet firmly touching the surface. If one foot is off the ground, the ladder may rock when you are near the top, causing you to slip or fall.

If the feet are on a hard surface such as a driveway or sidewalk, make sure they won't slip out when the ladder is leaned against a limb. One way is to glue or nail strips of rubber on the bottom of the feet. If you are planning to use your ladder in the garden where the soil is soft, first nail a board to each set of legs. This will prevent one or all of them from sinking down into the soil while you are on the ladder, which would put the ladder off balance and possibly throw you off.

When you are working at the top, never stand on the top step (even if you can brace yourself with your hands). Stay several rungs below and rest your thighs against the top step for added support. Do not lean out further than you can reach comfortably, or you may lose your balance and fall. And always face the ladder when climbing up or down.

Maintenance
When your ladder is not in use, keep it indoors or protected from the weather. Do not paint it—paint could hide any cracks in the wood, which would keep you from remedying them. Instead, rub linseed oil into the wood to keep it from drying out and splitting.

If the steps have bolts, check them occasionally to be sure they are tightened securely. If your ladder is broken, get rid of it and buy a new one.

It is not a good idea to store materials on a ladder; they can fall off much too easily.

CHAINSAWS

Parts of a Chainsaw

Anti-vibration cushions

Chain oiler

Compression release

Hand protector and chain break

Handle

Handle

Hand protector

Muffler

Engine in housing

Clutch and drive sprocket

Chain

Guide bar 12 to 25 inches long

Tip guard

Parts of a Chain

Cutter

Gullet

Side links

Center drive or link

Depth gauge

Chain direction

Bar slot or channel

Until recently, chainsaws were used primarily by loggers. But since the introduction of small, light models, including an electric version, the chainsaw has become a common household tool. Chainsaws can be used to cut firewood, to buck up (to cut wood into usable lengths) scrap wood in the backyard, and to prune trees. Special attachments can turn a chainsaw into a brush cutter, a hedge trimmer, a powerful winch, or a posthole digger.

A chainsaw, whether gas-powered or electric, has several major components: The engine to provide power; the clutch and drive sprocket to transfer the power; and the chain and guide bar that, together, form the cutting mechanism.

Chainsaws are sized primarily according to the length of the guide bars, which range from an impractical 8 inches long to the specialized 60-inch bar for bucking huge logs.

The two-cycle engines are rated by cubic-inch displacement, rather than by horsepower. Displacement is a formula involving the distance the piston moves on the stroke, the size of bore for the piston, and how much fuel-air mixture the piston compresses on its upward stroke. Thus, it is an indicator of power—the greater the displacement, the greater the power. For these tools, displacement varies from just 1.6 cubic inches on a mini-saw to 8.3 cubic inches on large production saws.

Parts of a Chain

A chain has several distinct parts, all linked together, the most important of which is the cutter head that slopes back slightly to reduce friction drag when mov-

ing through wood. Directly in front of the cutter (and part of the same link) is the depth gauge, which keeps the cutter from biting too deeply into the wood. Between these two elements is the gullet, which catches and removes the sawdust.

The correct height relationship between the cutter and the depth gauge is critical to a chain that cuts properly. Repeated sharpening causes the cutter to become shorter. When it does, the depth gauge must be filed down correspondingly. See page 60 for details on sharpening the chain.

The cutters normally are located on every other link, with the cutting edges facing in alternate directions. The cutting links are connected to each other by the drive links, which have hooked tangs that ride in the bar channel. The drive sprocket engages these tangs to turn the chain. Although the hooked part of the tang seems to be caught by the drive sprocket, it isn't—rather, the hook faces forward and is designed to keep the groove clear of sawdust.

There are four basic types of cutters. The rounded *chipper tooth* is most common. It can easily be sharpened with a round file.

The *chisel tooth* is much more efficient. It is square on top rather than round. This type is used most often by professionals; weekend cutters find it hard to do the more precise sharpening it requires.

The *semi-chisel tooth* is used on the average-quality saw with increasing frequency. This tooth design is a compromise between the chipper and the chisel tooth, and, like the chipper, the semi-chisel tooth can be sharpened with a round file.

The last type of tooth doesn't have a special name, but it is specifically for saws that have automatic sharpeners. Hand sharpening must be done in addition to the automatic sharpening and this hand sharpening is difficult to do correctly. Also, this type of chain is more expensive than the others.

The Guide Bar

The guide bar is what keeps the chain moving straight and smoothly. It is made of hardened steel to resist the great amount of wear it receives from the chain.

The tip of the bar is where most of the friction and resulting wear are centered. It is either made of specially hardened steel or protected by a nose sprocket that turns with the chain, reducing wear at that point.

The bar is grooved all the way around the edge; the sides of these grooves are called rails. The drive links of the chain ride on top of the rails, kept in place by the tangs in the channel.

Types of Chainsaw Cutters

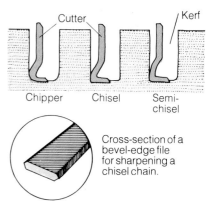

Cutter

Kerf

Chipper   Chisel   Semi-chisel

Cross-section of a bevel-edge file for sharpening a chisel chain.

What to Look For

It can be confusing to go shopping for a new chainsaw, especially if you've never bought one before.

First decide whether you want electric or gas. The electric saws are considerably cheaper, quieter, and easier to maintain, since there is no complex engine to look after. However, their bar lengths tend to be short (8 to 16 inches), which generally limits them to light work around the yard.

To cut a lot of firewood, you need a gas-engine chainsaw. A practical two-cycle gas-engine chainsaw has an engine with a 2.5 to 4.5-cubic-inch displacement and a 14 to 20-inch-long cutting bar.

There is a correlation between the size of the engine and the length of the cutting bar. The longer the bar, the bigger the engine must be in order to drive the chain effectively. The bar should be long enough to cut through most of the wood in only one pass. You can still cut larger logs by making two cuts, one from each side.

Modern chainsaws have several features that are worth insisting on. They are, in general order of priority, the following.

Solid-State Ignition

Increasingly, chainsaws are being made with solid-state ignition, which means that you don't need to periodically change the breaker points and condenser. This, in turn, means a big savings for you in time and effort.

Chain Brake

The brake is built into the forward handle and must be cocked before using. If the nose of the bar catches an obstruction and is flung up at your face, the jolt against the front handle activates the brake.

Tip Guard

This device actually prevents saw kick-back by enclosing the nose of the bar with a steel guard.

Antivibration Device

Rubber shock-absorbers called antivibration cushions are another common feature found on chainsaws. These devices reduce the vibration of the saw that would otherwise be transmitted to you.

Automatic Oiler

All good saws should have an automatic oiler. Because the oiler is geared to the engine speed, the faster the saw runs, the more oil it puts on the chain to reduce friction. The best system is an automatic oiler plus a manual override (pushing a small plunger with your thumb engages the override) because often the saw needs a little more oil than the automatic feed gives out.

Nose Sprocket

Look for a saw with a sprocket in the nose of the guide bar. The sprocket turns with the chain to markedly reduce friction at that point. These sprockets must be kept greased.

Compression Release

A particularly useful addition, especially on the larger saws, is a compression-release button. This button releases the compression that builds up in the engine as you pull the starter rope, making it easier for the engine to start.

Types of Chainsaws

Electric Chainsaw

These saws are mostly classified as mini-saws, but they also include light-duty models. They have bars that range from 8 to 16 inches long, with correspondingly larger motors for the longer bars. Since the cutting teeth tend to be smaller than on gas-engine saws, the cutting efficiency is reduced.

However, electric saws cost less than gas-powered saws. They are also quieter, as well as easier to start and maintain.

They do well at cutting up small logs, cutting heavy brush, or pruning tree limbs. As with all electric tools, however, your mobility is limited to areas within reach of a power outlet.

Gas-Engine Chainsaw

If you plan to cut one or more cords of wood for your fireplace each year, either a light- or medium-duty saw is a wise choice. Both are light, portable, and powerful. Choose the size that's best for you on the basis of how much and what size wood you plan to cut.

Power, which is determined by the engine's displacement, ranges from 2.5 to 4.5 cubic inches. Most of these saws can accept two to three different bar lengths, depending on the size of the engine. Bar lengths range from 12 inches on the smallest variety to 20 or 25 on the large models. For most cutting needs, a bar between 14 and 20 inches is sufficient.

Most of the new saws are equipped with two extremely useful accessories: (1) a chain brake and guard for safety and (2) an automatic oiler, plus a manual override for extra oil when needed.

Production Chainsaw

If you plan to cut a lot of firewood or build your own log cabin, you will need a production saw. These range in power from 4.5 cubic inches to more than 8 cubic inches, but a 6-cubic-inch engine will more than do for anyone who isn't a professional logger.

The bars on these saws usually run from 20 to 36 inches; a 25-inch bar is sufficient for most needs. On the larger saws, use a semi-chisel or chisel tooth chain for best cutting results. You can sharpen the chain by hand expertly on your own if you use a clamp-on file guide and a bevel-edged file.

Most of these saws are now made with a chain brake, an automatic oiler plus manual override, and a solid-state ignition.

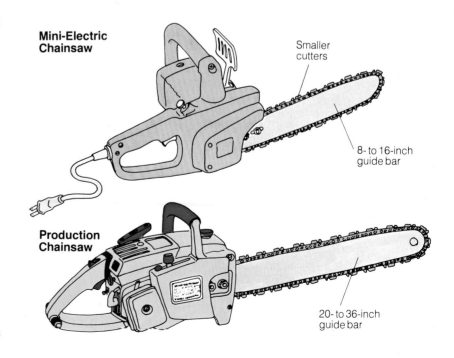

Mini-Electric Chainsaw

Smaller cutters

8- to 16-inch guide bar

Production Chainsaw

20- to 36-inch guide bar

Starting a Gasoline Chainsaw

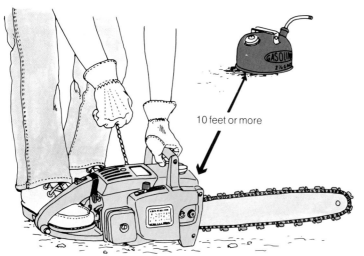

10 feet or more

Using a Chainsaw

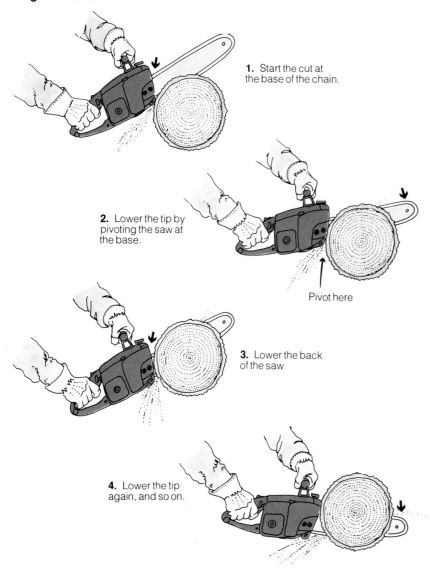

1. Start the cut at the base of the chain.

2. Lower the tip by pivoting the saw at the base.

Pivot here

3. Lower the back of the saw

4. Lower the tip again, and so on.

Chainsaw Safety

As you might imagine, a saw with a sharp chain that's moving at 50 feet per second is an inherently dangerous machine. However, if you use standard precautions and common sense, a chainsaw is no worse than a circular saw or any other power tool. These precautions are:

☐ In the woods, always wear a hard hat—there's a good reason why loose branches that fall from trees are called "widowmakers."

☐ Wear earplugs, even if you're only cutting for half an hour. The plugs reduce the saw's noise, which could otherwise damage your ear drums, while still allowing you to hear people talking or shouting. Some hard hats are conveniently equipped with built-in ear plugs.

☐ When starting the saw, keep 10 feet away from the fuel to prevent the risk of explosion or fire.

☐ When starting the saw, place it securely on the ground in a cleared area, and make sure the bar is not contacting anything. Before pulling the starter rope, put one hand on the front handle and a foot through the rear handle.

☐ When bucking up logs (cutting fallen trees into logs), first remove any limbs or nearby brush that may catch the tip of the saw and cause it to kick back at you.

☐ Always stand on the uphill side of the log, particularly when bucking a log that's lying across a steep slope.

☐ When falling a tree, make sure you know which way it's going to fall—and make sure it won't fall on your car or truck. Also make sure you have a clear path away from the tree when it begins to fall, so that you can get well out of its way.

☐ Always keep your head and body out of line with the chain and bar when cutting. Otherwise the chain might hit something and kick back at you.

☐ Never work with the saw raised above chest height; this level brings the chain too close to your throat and face.

☐ Never walk around with the saw still running.

Maintenance

Cleaning

With the engine turned off, wipe the engine housing and chain bar with a clean rag. Then wipe the bar with an oily rag and lightly coat the chain with oil.

Storage

Before putting your chainsaw into storage for any amount of time, remove the oil-gas mixture. Run the engine with the choke open until no fuel remains. Cover the chain to protect it from grit.

Adjusting Chain Tension

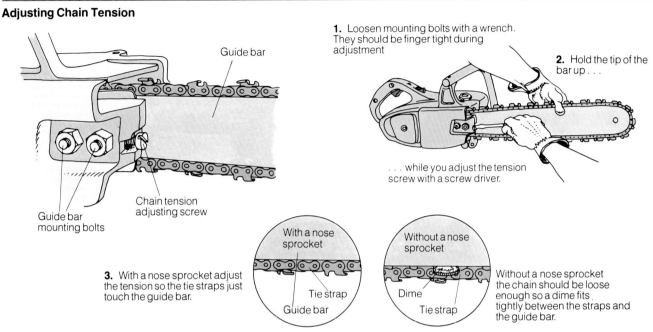

Guide bar

1. Loosen mounting bolts with a wrench. They should be finger tight during adjustment

2. Hold the tip of the bar up . . .

. . . while you adjust the tension screw with a screw driver.

Chain tension adjusting screw

Guide bar mounting bolts

3. With a nose sprocket adjust the tension so the tie straps just touch the guide bar.

With a nose sprocket

Tie strap

Guide bar

Without a nose sprocket

Dime

Tie strap

Without a nose sprocket the chain should be loose enough so a dime fits tightly between the straps and the guide bar.

See pages 77–95 for details about engine maintenance. Also consult your owner's manual.

Chain and Guide Bar Maintenance
The chain and guide bar require just as much attention as the engine, if not more. The chain tension must be carefully adjusted; the chain must be properly sharpened; the nose sprocket (if there is one) must be kept greased; and the bar must be inspected regularly for any wear or damage. Neglecting any of these elements will cause the saw to cut incorrectly and, ultimately, to be ruined.

Adjusting Chain Tension
The chain must be kept properly adjusted for efficient cutting. A too-tight chain will overheat and break or damage the bar; a too-loose chain will cut poorly, damage the bar, and possibly fly off the bar.

Because a chain expands slightly as it warms up, adjust the tension only when the chain is cool. To do this, first make sure

the ignition is off. Then loosen the bar-mounting nuts so that the chain tension screw can move the bar. Hold the nose of the bar up, then tighten the chain tension screw until the tie straps on each link just touch the bottom of the bar. Pull the chain around several times, holding the nose up all the while. If the tie straps are still just barely touching the bar, tighten the bar-mounting nuts. (If your saw does not have a nose sprocket, there should be enough room for the edge of a dime between the tie straps and the bar bottom.)

The chain will sag slightly when it is warm from use, but it should sag no more than half the depth of the tang in the groove. If it still sags this much after the chain has cooled, retighten the bar-mounting nuts.

Always consult your owner's manual when you do any work on your equipment.

The Guide Bar
The guide bar must be inspected and cleaned regularly. Each time you clean the

saw, brush out the channel with an old toothbrush. Use a sharpened twig to remove any dirt that's stuck inside.

To make sure the rails are even and straight, sight down the channels from the nose of the saw. If you see that the rails are spread out at the top, you can hammer them back into shape. Place the bar on a flat, hard surface and put a length of 1 by 4 on the side of the rail. Hammer the wood lightly to bring the rail back in line.

Every time you remove the chain to work on the saw, turn the bar over. This regular rotation will keep the bar from becoming too worn on one side.

If the bar has a nose sprocket, it should be greased each time you use the saw. With a small needle-nose grease gun (available from most chainsaw dealers), pump in grease until you see the grease oozing out around the sprocket.

A final note on preventive maintenance: When the bar is pinched in a cut, never twist and jerk it to get it free. Instead, pry the log up or use wedges.

Evening the Rails on the Guide Bar

Place a 1x4 block over rails that are spread out, and hammer the block to bring the rails into line.

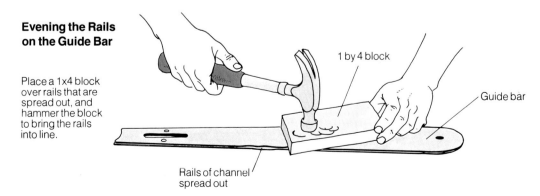

1 by 4 block

Guide bar

Rails of channel spread out

Sharpening the Chain

Tools

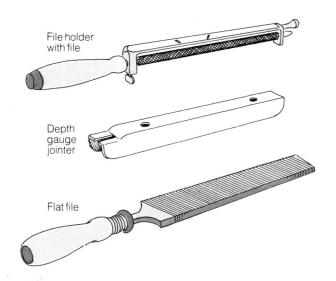

File holder
with file

Depth
gauge
jointer

Flat file

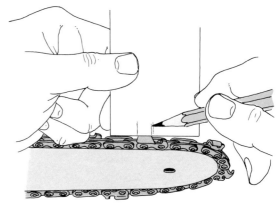

1. Find the shortest cutter. Mark the length on a piece of paper and compare it with others. Mark the shortest with a pencil so you can find it later.

2. After tightening the chain to its proper tension, sharpen the shortest cutter first and the others to match. Hold the file at a 35-degree angle using the marks on the holder. File from the inside to the outside of each cutter.

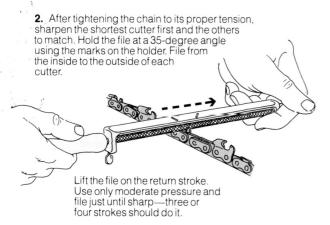

Lift the file on the return stroke. Use only moderate pressure and file just until sharp—three or four strokes should do it.

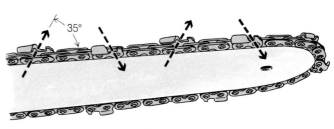

35°

3. Sharpen all the cutters on one side. Turn the saw around and do the other side.

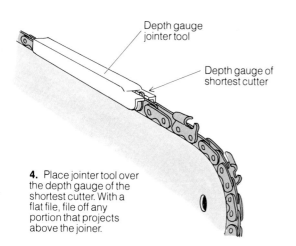

Depth gauge jointer tool

Depth gauge of shortest cutter

4. Place jointer tool over the depth gauge of the shortest cutter. With a flat file, file off any portion that projects above the joiner.

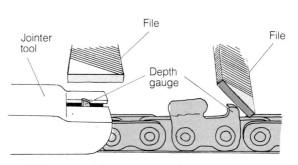

Jointer tool

File

File

Depth gauge

5. Remove the jointer and round off the leading edge of the depth gauge as it was before you filed off the top.

POWERED LOG-SPLITTING DEVICES

If you will be splitting several cords of wood a year, you can do it the traditional way with a sledgehammer and wedge, or with a splitting maul. For more information on these methods, see ORTHO's book *Energy-Saving Projects for the Home*. On the other hand, you can also make use of more modern advances by choosing either of two different types of powered splitters that will make your work a lot easier.

One type is a hydraulic splitting ram that delivers anywhere from 7 to 15 tons of force, depending on its size. The other type is a giant screw that bolts to the rear wheel hub of your car. Although it is slower than a ram, it is considerably cheaper.

Types of Powered Log-Splitting Devices

Hydraulic Log Splitter
The hydraulic log splitter is essentially a gas-engine and hydraulic-power unit mounted on a steel trailer frame that has a steel wedge welded near the front of the trailer tongue. The log is placed in front of the wedge; when the ram is released, it forces the log into the wedge and splits it.

Screw-Type Splitter
This device, which is powered by your car or truck, simply screws its way into a log and forces the log apart. (One model has the patented trade name of The Stickler.)

To use this splitter, jack the car up and remove the left rear wheel (or, on front-wheel-drive cars, the left front wheel). An adapter plate allows you to bolt the splitter onto the hub of virtually any vehicle, whether domestic or imported.

When you turn the engine on and put it in gear, the screw will spin. To split the log, just jam it against the tip of the screw. One end of the log catches on the ground while the splitter begins turning its way into the log.

Maintenance
Taking care of a hydraulic log splitter primarily involves keeping the four-cycle engine maintained and tuned. See pages 77–86 for instructions.

Log Splitters

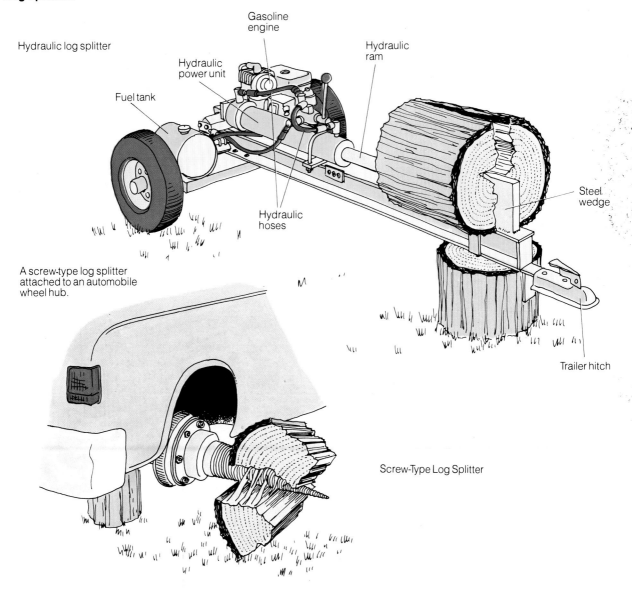

Hydraulic log splitter

Gasoline engine

Hydraulic power unit

Hydraulic ram

Fuel tank

Hydraulic hoses

Steel wedge

Trailer hitch

A screw-type log splitter attached to an automobile wheel hub.

Screw-Type Log Splitter

WATERING AND PEST CONTROL

Watering cans, hoses, sprinklers, sprayers, dusters—this chapter tells you how to select the best quality tools and accessories, repair hoses, trouble-shoot sprayers, and keep all your watering and pest control equipment in good condition.

The cause of improper watering, more often than not, is confusion about *how much* to water and *how often* to water. If you ask 100 gardeners for advice on this subject, each one probably will give you a different answer—and the trouble is that they may all be at least partially right.

The best practice is to water enough to wet the soil to the bottom of the plants' root zones. You need to understand your soil type in order to determine how much water the soil particles can retain.

For details on soil /water relationships, see ORTHO's *All About Fertilizers, Soils & Water*.

The best way to figure out how often to apply water to a lawn or garden is to observe carefully. Give it a good watering and then get down on your hands and knees. With a trowel, dig several inches to a foot into the soil. The soil around the root level should be quite wet at this time; later, just before it's time to water again, this soil should be just moist; and in between waterings, the moisture level of the soil should be somewhere in the middle.

What's important is to get the water down to the root zone, which varies in depth according to the type of plant. A lawn, for example, must be watered down to the grass roots on a regular basis; trees, however, may require long, deep, but infrequent soakings.

The basic rule is: Water *thoroughly*. You may be having a good time standing out there with a hose in your hand spraying the garden or lawn, but if you don't have the patience to stand there long enough to apply sufficient water, you might actually be doing more harm than good. When water penetrates only a few inches down, shallow (rather than deep) root growth is encouraged. The plant then suffers—and you anguish because nothing seems to grow well.

Watering Cans and Roses

Sprinkling cans aren't just for watering plants—they also can be used to apply liquid fertilizers and some types of herbicides that are diluted with water. And when not in use, or when worn beyond repair, they can be converted into decorative flower pots.

Cans come in various sizes, shapes, and materials. They are made of plastic and metal (e.g., copper, brass, or galvanized steel). Plastic watering cans are used most widely—they are inexpensive, durable, and rust resistant.

Galvanized steel cans have been around for years and are still the favorite of many gardeners. They are durable, rust resistant, and usually more expensive than plastic cans.

Brass and copper watering cans are practical, beautiful—and expensive. However, if kept clean and dry when not in use, they will last a lifetime. They also make especially attractive flower pots.

Just as durable and nearly as decorative as the copper can is the steel can that's covered with an enameled epoxy coating, usually in a bright color.

Just as important as the can itself is the nozzle, or *rose*, at the end of the spout. This distributes the water gently and evenly. Roses are generally oval or round

Selecting a Watering Can— What to Look For

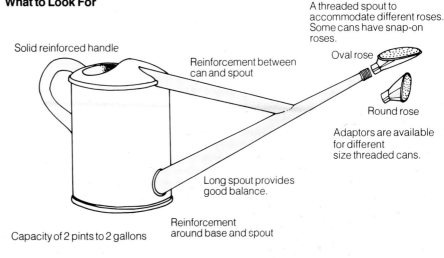

Solid reinforced handle

Reinforcement between can and spout

A threaded spout to accommodate different roses. Some cans have snap-on roses.

Oval rose

Round rose

Adaptors are available for different size threaded cans.

Long spout provides good balance.

Capacity of 2 pints to 2 gallons

Reinforcement around base and spout

Proper spraying helps control pests and keeps your garden beautiful.

and face either up or out. They are made of plastic, brass, or copper and can screw on or clamp on. Some roses have adapters so they will fit on other-size models.

For seedlings, the oval-shape rose that points upward is best. It allows the water to come out in a gentle rain that won't disturb the soil around seedlings and young plants.

The round rose is for older plants. It points out or slightly down from the spout and puts out a greater volume of water, which suits the hardier older plants. If you need a gentle flow of water for seedlings, use a rose with a rubber bulb attached; it puts out a very fine shower.

A long spout generally makes for good balance. Pick up the can: If it feels well balanced when empty, it probably will also feel that way when it's full.

Look for a can that has a threaded tip —it can accept different types of roses. Cans that are made with a one-piece spout and rose tend to be cheaper, but, because the holes are less well made, the cans also are less efficient.

Finally, look for reinforcement around areas of stress, such as the can's bottom, the handle, and the seam between the body and the spout.

Maintenance

Drain watering cans whenever they aren't in use, and store them upside down. When possible, keep the plastic varieties out of the sun's ultraviolet rays.

If possible, periodically remove the roses to clean them of sediment. Rinse them by running water back through the holes from the front. Use a toothpick to clean out any stubborn particles.

HOSES

A well-made hose consists of three main parts: The skin (outer section); several inner layers (plys); and the central core that actually carries the water.

Hose-construction materials include rubber, nylon, vinyl, and plastic. In many cases, two or more of these materials are combined.

Whether you choose a hose of rubber or of vinyl and nylon, look for good quality. A cheap hose that kinks easily will soon crack and will give you nothing but frustration.

Plys. Hoses normally are rated according to three categories—"good," "better," and "best." The distinguishing factor has to do with the number and quality of plys (inner layers). A "best"-quality rubber hose, for example, has a core made of an extra-heavy rubber inner tube, which is wrapped with two layers of synthetic mesh fiber and then covered with a rubber outer skin. A "better" rubber hose, on the other hand, includes a light- to medium-weight rubber tube wrapped with one layer of synthetic mesh and covered with a rubber skin. And a "good" hose may cost 50 percent less than a "best" one, so if you don't need all those superior features you can save some money by compromising on a "better" hose.

Even when considering vinyl and nylon hoses, make sure that you buy one with several plys for added strength. The price reflects the number of the plys.

Couplings. Also check the couplings. Solid brass couplings are best—they are strong and rust proof. Select those brass couplings with an octagonal shape for ease in tightening and loosening. This type of coupling is cast rather than extruded and stamped, which makes it more durable; if you can't find a hose with this type of coupling, your next choice should be round brass, then galvanized steel. Plastic is the last (and least) choice. When you need to make repairs, buy replacement parts made of the octagonal, cast-brass type.

Diameter. There's also the diameter of the hose to consider. Five basic sizes usually are sold: ⅜-inch diameter, ½-inch diameter, ⅝-inch diameter, ¾-inch diameter, and 1-inch diameter. The ⅜- and ½-inch-diameter sizes are used for watering container plants; the ⅝-inch size is most popular for lawns and gardens; and the ¾- and 1-inch hoses are used for very large yards, commercial greenhouses, nurseries, or small farms.

The smaller the diameter, the less water the hose will deliver in a given period. You might not think there was much difference between a ½-inch hose and a ⅝-inch

Styles of Watering Cans

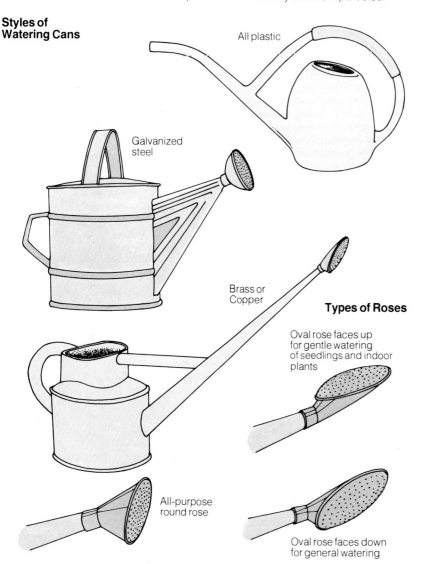

All plastic

Galvanized steel

Brass or Copper

Types of Roses

Oval rose faces up for gentle watering of seedlings and indoor plants

All-purpose round rose

Oval rose faces down for general watering

Anatomy of a Garden Hose

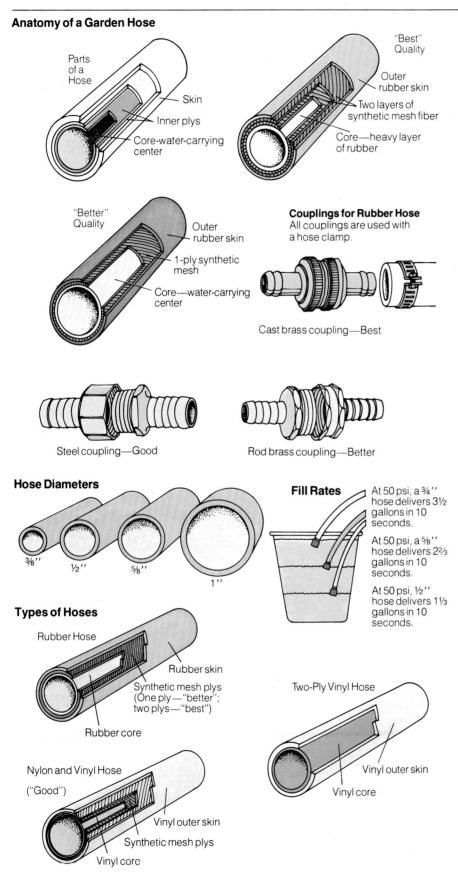

Parts of a Hose
- Skin
- Inner plys
- Core-water-carrying center

"Best" Quality
- Outer rubber skin
- Two layers of synthetic mesh fiber
- Core—heavy layer of rubber

"Better" Quality
- Outer rubber skin
- 1-ply synthetic mesh
- Core—water-carrying center

Couplings for Rubber Hose
All couplings are used with a hose clamp.

Cast brass coupling—Best

Steel coupling—Good

Rod brass coupling—Better

Hose Diameters

⅜'' ½'' ⅝'' 1''

Fill Rates

At 50 psi, a ¾'' hose delivers 3½ gallons in 10 seconds.

At 50 psi, a ⅝'' hose delivers 2⅔ gallons in 10 seconds.

At 50 psi, ½'' hose delivers 1⅓ gallons in 10 seconds.

Types of Hoses

Rubber Hose
- Rubber skin
- Synthetic mesh plys (One ply—"better"; two plys—"best")
- Rubber core

Nylon and Vinyl Hose ("Good")
- Vinyl outer skin
- Synthetic mesh plys
- Vinyl core

Two-Ply Vinyl Hose
- Vinyl outer skin
- Vinyl core

---

hose, but consider this: In 10 seconds, at 50 psi, a ½-inch hose delivers 1⅓ gallons of water; a ⅝-inch hose delivers 2⅔ gallons; and a ¾-inch hose delivers 3⅓ gallons. Clearly, when you need a large amount of water delivered, larger hoses will save you time.

Types of Hoses

Rubber Hoses
Rubber hoses generally are considered to be best. Although they are slightly heavier than other types, they offer years of service and dependability. They also resist cold weather, sun damage, and abrasion. Some top-quality rubber hoses can take up to 600 psi, although normally "best" hoses tend to tolerate a standard of between 150 and 200 psi. However, this is still well within the limits of normal household pressure, which runs between 30 and 50 psi. Good rubber hoses also stay flexible in very cold weather (from 0° to −35°F, depending on their rating) and withstand hot water up to 160°F.

Nylon and Vinyl Hoses
Nylon and vinyl hoses have become increasingly popular recently, due to improvements in construction quality. Good nylon and vinyl hoses (generally, both materials are used in combination) are flexible even down to 0°F and will withstand up to 500 psi. Not only are they lighter than the rubber hoses but they are also generally cheaper, sometimes by more than 50 percent. However, the cheaper models of this type tend to kink more easily than a rubber hose. Once kinked, they do not readily round out again, which reduces the water flow at that point. Vinyl hoses also are more subject to the deteriorating effects of ultraviolet sun rays.

Two-Ply Vinyl Hose
If you want a long-lasting hose, do *not* buy this nonreinforced type. Retailers often sell two-ply vinyl hoses at very low prices as advertising. If these hoses are subjected to pressure for any length of time, they are likely to break. They also kink easily and are difficult to roll up.

Maintenance
In caring for a hose, one of the first rules is: Never let it kink. Any kink becomes a weak point, and the hose will tend to kink there repeatedly. Not only will this restrict water flow but it will finally make the hose crack in that spot. Also, don't shut off the line while there is pressure in it. If you have a nozzle that allows you to shut off the water flow while the spigot is turned on, use it only when you must—and then never for long periods of time.

When you hang a hose, put it on a proper support or reel (see next section). Do not put it on a nail, or it will sag and kink.

Keep the hose out of the sun. Eventually, the sun's ultraviolet rays will damage any hose, particularly those made of nylon and vinyl.

At the end of the season, drain the hose and hang it properly in a dry area.

Hose Reels and Hangers

Hanging up a hose properly will greatly extend its life. "Proper" hanging means keeping it kink-free, off the ground, and out of the sun when not in use. The best way to accomplish all this is to use a hose reel or hanger. A hose that's left to lie out on the lawn, sidewalk, or driveway invites injury —someone might trip over it— and driving your car over either end of the hose will damage the coupling.

There is a cheap, convenient solution, in the form of a simple hose hanger that screws to the basement or garage wall. But before making an actual purchase, check the length and size of the hose you plan to hang on it. Some hangers will handle 250 feet of ½-inch hose or 150 feet of ⅝-inch hose. The heavy-duty models will hold 300 feet of ½-inch hose and 200 feet of ⅝-inch hose. If you have several hoses, buy two or three hangers rather than trying to overload a single one.

A swivel-mounted hose reel that attaches to the wall makes it convenient to unreel a hose. This hose reel is usually mounted next to the hose bib (spigot). The reel has a handle on it for turning; when not in use, the reel swings flat against the wall. Most of these types will handle 100 feet of ⅝-inch hose.

The hose reel-and-cart combination works best for moving the hose around the lawn or garden. One convenient model is pushed upright on its wheels; then, when it's time to reel the hose out or in, the cart is tilted over onto its handle for more stability.

Hose Repairs

Occasionally a hose gets worn and develops a leak or a coupling gets bent and becomes unusable. You don't have to throw the hose away, however—you can repair it for a fraction of what it would cost to buy a new one. You can find hose-repair kits for mending a cut section of the hose or for replacing couplings (both male and female).

If the hose has a pinhole leak, make a temporary repair with a wooden toothpick and some plastic electrical tape. Push the tip of the toothpick into the hole, just through the thickness of the hose wall. Then break off the toothpick flush with the outer skin. When the wood gets wet through normal use, it will swell, thereby

Hose Storage

Place hoses on proper support or reel to prevent kinks. Keep hoses out of the sun.

Wall-mounted swivel hose reel

Hose reel mounted on a cart for transporting around the garden

**Hose Repair
Plugging a Pinhole Leak**

Round toothpick

1. Locate the leak

2. Push the tip of a tooth pick into the hole, just through the thickness of the hose wall. Break off the toothpick flush with the outer skin. The wood will swell when wet, firmly plugging the hole.

Electrical tape

Former leak

3. Wrap electrical tape about 2 inches beyond each side of the hole. Stretch tape tightly over the hole but not at the ends. This allows flexibility.

firmly plugging the hole. Now wrap the hose with electrical tape about 2 inches beyond each side of the hole. Stretch the tape tightly over the hole but not on either end; this allows the tape to expand if the hose is bent near the puncture point.

For larger holes or cuts, as well as for more permanent repairs, use a hose-repair kit. These kits include repair parts made of solid brass or plastic (brass is best if your hose is a good one).

There are two basic types of repair kits: (1) a permanent brass clincher and (2) a

reusable brass or high-impact plastic insert. The size of the brass clinchers must suit the diameter of your hose; the reusable inserts fit most hoses between ½ and ¾ inches. However, check the specifications on the repair package (both types of kits come with detailed instructions and illustrations).

The male and female couplings are also sold separately, which enables you to replace a coupling on the end of the hose. This replacement is done the same way as for mending a hose in the middle.

NOZZLES AND HEADS

Repair Devices

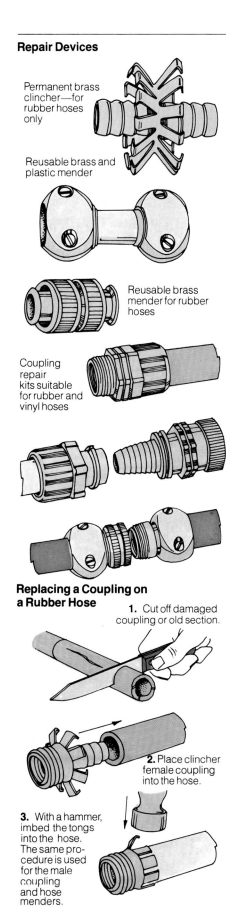

Permanent brass clincher—for rubber hoses only

Reusable brass and plastic mender

Reusable brass mender for rubber hoses

Coupling repair kits suitable for rubber and vinyl hoses

Replacing a Coupling on a Rubber Hose

1. Cut off damaged coupling or old section.

2. Place clincher female coupling into the hose.

3. With a hammer, imbed the tongs into the hose. The same procedure is used for the male coupling and hose menders.

A nozzle offers a variety of advantages: you don't have to kink the end of the hose when you want to temporarily stop the flow of water; you don't have to strain your thumb to create a hard stream of water; and you can change the water from a soft rain to a concentrated stream. Also, the wide array of heads available lets you accomplish a multitude of jobs.

Nozzles and heads are made of several different materials. Solid brass is best, followed by brass-plated zinc, followed by plastic (this is adequate but less durable than the other types). You may wish to choose several nozzles and heads; they save a lot of labor and don't cost too much money.

Types of Nozzles

Twist-Control Nozzle

This adjustable nozzle has been the standard for years. Shifting the dial on the tip changes the flow of water from a fine spray to a hard stream.

Both brass and plastic models are available. On some quality brass models, the front stem can be unscrewed and removed to expose the base, which provides a direct, higher-volume stream of water.

The plastic models cost less than the brass, and the better ones are insulated to protect your hand from either hot or cold water.

Pistol-Grip Nozzle

Pistol-grip nozzles are available in brass-plated zinc and plastic. The pistol grip and trigger make it easy to hold and change the spray type with one hand. Squeezing the trigger controls the volume of water and, therefore, the pattern of spray. To keep the volume at a certain level, just turn a knurled knob near the trigger. The next time the trigger is squeezed, it will instantly produce the preset volume. Some models have a stainless steel clip that locks the trigger. This relieves the strain on your hand, which can be a problem with this type of nozzle.

Some pistol-grip sprayers have an adjustment for water volume in the nozzle. On some models, the tips are threaded to accept other attachments, such as fan sprayers, water wands, and proportioners (these feed out specific amounts of liquid fertilizer from an attached container).

Sweeper or Cleaning Nozzles

Patterned after the firefighting hose, these nozzles are used to direct large volumes of water in powerful streams. They are short, tapered, and not adjustable. Their main use is for cleaning driveways, walks, exterior walls, and garden statues and for clearing leaves from lawns.

Spray Nozzles

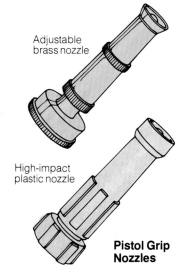

Adjustable brass nozzle

High-impact plastic nozzle

Pistol Grip Nozzles

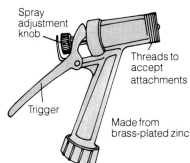

Spray adjustment knob

Trigger

Threads to accept attachments

Made from brass-plated zinc

High-impact plastic pistol grip nozzle

Sweeper or Cleaning Nozzles

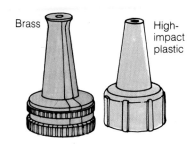

Brass

High-impact plastic

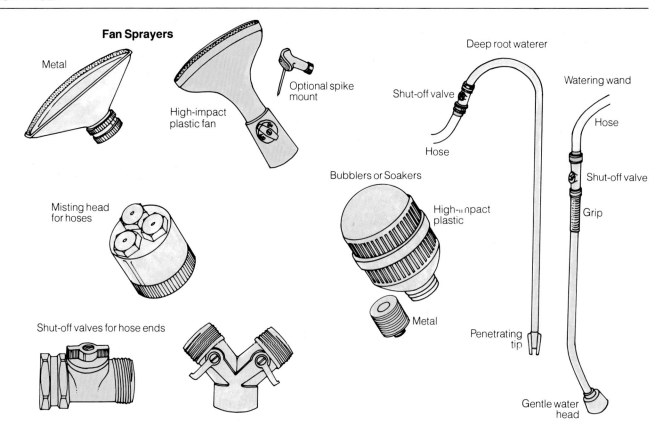

Fan Sprayers

Metal

High-impact plastic fan

Optional spike mount

Misting head for hoses

Shut-off valves for hose ends

Deep root waterer

Shut-off valve

Hose

Bubblers or Soakers

High-impact plastic

Metal

Watering wand

Hose

Shut-off valve

Grip

Penetrating tip

Gentle water head

Types of Heads

Fan-Spray Heads
This type is an excellent choice for watering seedlings, delicate border-garden flowers, or flower boxes. The head produces a wide spray with a fairly high volume of water, but its delivery is more gentle than that of pistol-grip or twist-control nozzles.

These heads tend to be made entirely of plastic, but some have a brass watering head that's set in plastic.

Another feature is a swivel-mounted spike that holds the head in the lawn for heavy, direct watering. The spike snaps under the handle when not in use.

Bubblers, or Soaker Heads
These are good accessories for doing gentle watering. Shaped like a bulb or small ball, bubblers screw onto the end of the hose. They mix the water with air to deliver a high volume of water without eroding the soil. These bubblers are ideal for deep watering, soaking, or filling irrigation ditches for vegetable gardens—just put the nozzle on the ground. However, some types can also be adjusted to shoot a straight stream or deliver a gentle spray.

Misting Heads
Misting heads put out a fine, foglike spray and are especially useful in greenhouses for watering tropical foliage plants. The sprays may adjust from a coarse-but-delicate spray to a fine mist. The better heads are made of brass and have removable jets for periodic cleaning.

Other Hose Accessories

Hose-End Valves
When a head (e.g., a bubbler) lacks a shut-off device, consider buying one—it will save you trips to and from the spigot. Constructed of plastic, zinc, or brass, these valves have a female end for connecting to the hose and a male end for attaching the accessories. A ball valve located inside is operated by a lever to control the flow of water.

Wands
Hose-extender wands are excellent aids to water shrubs or hanging plants in hard-to-reach spots. They are also useful in greenhouses where seedlings may be located far back on the plant bench.

The handles can be up to 48 inches long. Most are made of aluminum, with a hand grip of soft vinyl or rubber.

The better wands have a threaded tip, which lets you remove a damaged nozzle or other accessory head to clean or replace it. Some wands also have shut-off valves built in so you don't end up inadvertently watering the floor or ground between the potted plants.

Root Waterers
Root waterers are used to get water and fertilizer deep into the ground next to tree roots. This tool is a long steel tube with a series of holes near the sharpened bottom and a hose connection at the top. Many root waterers have a chamber at the top, in which a fertilizer cartridge is placed. The water flows through the cartridge, dilutes the fertilizer, and carries the solution to the roots.

These waterers are especially useful in areas with compacted soil that keeps water away from the roots. Just insert the root waterer at the tree's drip line (the limits of the branch extension). Use moderate water pressure and move the waterer 6 to 8 feet every hour or so until you have worked your way around the tree.

Maintenance
To maintain nozzles, heads, and hose accessories, check periodically to see that the holes (jets) are not clogged. If they are, unplug them. After each job, rinse the entire unit so that it is completely cleared of soil and debris.

SPRINKLERS

It isn't easy to decide on a sprinkler—there are so many kinds to choose from. Some throw water in a round, rectangular, or square pattern; others revolve, oscillate, or pulsate. Then there's the traveling sprinkler, which looks like a toy tractor crawling around the grass. You can even get a sprinkler that obligingly rolls up the hose behind it and shuts itself off when done.

To some degree, however, your choice is predetermined by the size and shape of the area to be covered and by the existence or nonexistence of trees that might block the water pattern. If you have a large piece of land, it's best to measure it, then transfer the dimensions to graph paper so that your planning will be accurate.

Obtain manufacturers' specifications for a variety of sprinklers. See if the water patterns of these sprinklers match the area you want watered. Take into account how quickly your soil type absorbs water. Don't buy a sprinkler that puts out water so fast that most of it runs off into the gutter. Impulse sprinklers have the most versatile patterns. They and revolving sprinklers can be height-adjusted to cover the area under trees. If your yard is so large that individual sprinklers won't achieve adequate coverage, you can opt for an underground system.

Types of Sprinklers

There are four basic types of sprinklers: fixed, oscillating, revolving, and impulse.

Fixed Sprinkler

The fixed sprinkler has no moving parts. It is generally used to cover small to medium-size areas. The pattern of holes in the head resembles the rose on a watering can and enables the sprinkler to make a round, rectangular, square, fan-shape, or narrow-band pattern. Some models contain four different heads in one sprinkler; you just dial the desired pattern. A fixed sprinkler is excellent for covering hard-to-reach corners of the yard or small reseeded areas that need more water than the rest of the lawn.

Oscillating Sprinkler

This type throws a long, rectangular pattern from a single, 12 to 20-inch-long tube that contains 14 to 20 nozzle openings. The sprinkler can be adjusted so that the water is thrown in any of three positions: (1) fully, from right to left and back; (2) just from the center to the left or the right; or (3) from a stationary position.

In good oscillating sprinklers, the nozzles are made of brass and they screw into the tube individually. They can be removed for cleaning or replaced if necessary. On less expensive models, the nozzles are permanently set into the tube.

Revolving Sprinkler

Revolving sprinklers have two or more arms that spin because of the pressure of the water. The arms are made of either plastic or brass, although the housing tends to be plastic. Some revolving sprinklers have two wheels or skids so that they can be pulled around the lawn easily.

The better models have adjustable nozzle tips on the revolving arms. This feature allows you to vary the height and width of the watering pattern, which ranges from 5 to 50 feet. The long, low pattern permits broad coverage under hanging tree limbs.

Impulse Sprinkler

This sprinkler, with its familiar "tocka-tocka" sound, rotates when the water strikes a counterbalanced and spring-activated arm. The water strikes the arm and is broken into small particles rather than a solid stream. Then the arm swings out from the force of the water; the spring mechanism snaps it back, causing the sprinkler mechanism to move and change the direction of the water spray slightly.

The arms can also be locked into position to water a narrow strip.

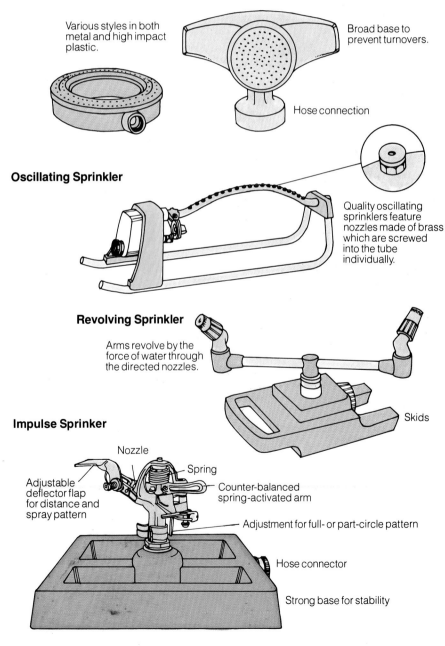

Fixed Sprinklers

Various styles in both metal and high impact plastic.

Broad base to prevent turnovers.

Hose connection

Oscillating Sprinkler

Quality oscillating sprinklers feature nozzles made of brass which are screwed into the tube individually.

Revolving Sprinkler

Arms revolve by the force of water through the directed nozzles.

Skids

Impulse Sprinker

Nozzle

Spring

Adjustable deflector flap for distance and spray pattern

Counter-balanced spring-activated arm

Adjustment for full- or part-circle pattern

Hose connector

Strong base for stability

FAUCET ACCESSORIES

Traveling Sprinklers

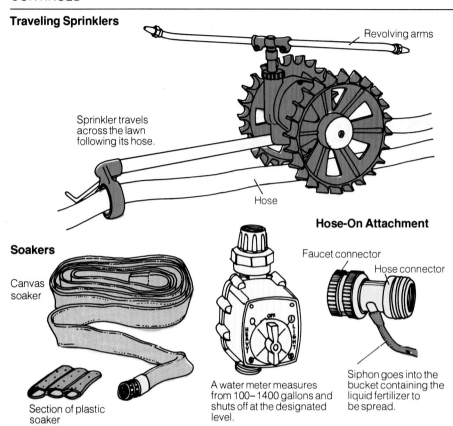

Revolving arms

Sprinkler travels across the lawn following its hose.

Hose

Soakers

Canvas soaker

Section of plastic soaker

Hose-On Attachment

Faucet connector

Hose connector

A water meter measures from 100–1400 gallons and shuts off at the designated level.

Siphon goes into the bucket containing the liquid fertilizer to be spread.

This process repeats over and over.

These sprinklers can be set to cover a full circle or a narrow, fan-shape pattern. Several different sizes of nozzles are available, allowing you to control the amount of water that's put out. Impulse sprinklers will sprinkle a circle up to 100 feet in diameter, depending on the water pressure and nozzle size.

On some models, the nozzles can also be adjusted for either low or high-level streams. The long, low level is for reaching under hanging limbs of trees.

Traveling Sprinklers

These also use the revolving arm system and are great for people with little time to do their own watering. You can start a traveling sprinkler before you go to work in the morning. It will slowly make its way around the lawn and then shut itself off.

There are two basic types: (1) a toy-tractorlike sprinkler that drags the hose and (2) a sprinkler that looks like a hose reel and rolls up the hose as it moves along.

Both types follow the hose pattern that's laid out on the lawn. Both are powered by the water pressure, which turns wheel gears. The size and length of the hose and its corresponding weight influence how far these sprinklers can travel—that is, between 75 and 300 feet. Naturally, this distance affects the total coverage, which

can be 20,000 square feet or more. Coverage also is influenced by how the nozzles are adjusted; these adjustments can vary the circle pattern of the rotating-type sprinkler from 10 to 50 feet in diameter. For details on individual models, check manufacturer's specifications.

Soaker Hoses

A soaker hose is a length of hose that seeps water. A loosely woven *canvas hose* was the original soaker hose and it is still available. The porous canvas allows water to ooze through all along its length. The water pressure must be adjusted at the hose bib so that the force of the water doesn't enlarge the hose's pores. Otherwise, the water will emerge from these enlarged pores at a faster rate in the future. Canvas hoses usually rot after one season's use and must be replaced. However, if the hose is picked up and dried after each use, it will last longer.

Recently, plastic and rubber soaker hoses have been developed. These work like the canvas hoses, but they do not rot. However, too much pressure can still damage them.

Soaker hoses are excellent for watering long rows (as in vegetable gardens), narrow borders, or hedges. Most gardeners find it convenient to leave the hose in position all season and to attach a garden hose to it when it is needed.

Use your hose bib to attach devices that will save you money and time: a *water meter* that shuts off the watering system automatically, or *hose-ons* that mix fertilizer with water in the hose.

Water Meters

Often called water timers, these devices are more accurately termed meters since they measure the amount of water passing through. They can be set at any of 48 different positions for high to low volumes of water. The old water timers, which actually had a clock mechanism, didn't ensure an even amount of water (a drop in water pressure meant less water, which the clock timer couldn't take into account). The new flow meters are not affected by pressure drops.

The meter package includes suggestions for settings to use with different types of sprinklers from different manufacturers.

Some models have two different settings: (1) one setting will deliver up to 1,600 gallons of water and then shut off automatically and (2) the other setting lets you bypass the automatic shutoff, providing a continuous flow. If you choose a model with only one setting, you won't have the bypass option. And there's another model with an antihammer valve to protect the water pipes. ("Hammer" is the rattling of pipes that happens when water flow is suddenly stopped, causing a sharp pressure increase in the pipes.)

Hose-Ons

The hose-on device is another useful faucet accessory. Usually made of brass, it proportions liquid or soluble fertilizer into the water that flows through the hose. One end has a female fitting to screw onto the hose bib; the other end has a male fitting to accept the hose. A small rubber hose runs from a short brass nipple extending from the bottom of the hose-on to a bucket of fertilizer mixed with water. Water passing through the hose-on draws the liquid fertilizer from the bucket by forming a vacuum in the device. The hose-on dilutes the solution in the bucket at a rate of 16 parts water to 1 part solution. Therefore, the ratio of fertilizer to water that leaves the end of the hose depends on what concentration of solution you put in the bucket. Because the dilution rate is 16:1, put 1 cup of solution per gallon of water in the bucket for every tablespoon of solution per gallon of water that you want to come out of the end of the hose. (There are 16 tablespoons in a cup.)

When you are finished, clean the device by drawing some fresh water in the bucket up and through the hose-on. Then hang it up so the small brass tube is pointing up. This will drain all water from inside.

PEST CONTROL

How can you fend off pests? There are countless ways. Some involve pesticides and some don't.

You can buy biological pest controls in nurseries. There are fungi that will attack the larvae of such pests as Japanese beetles or leaf-eating caterpillars. You can also buy natural insect predators such as ladybugs and praying mantises, but they usually don't remain in your garden long enough to do much good.

One of the best ways to keep bugs under control is to spend a lot of time in the garden watching for them, so that you can spot potential problems before they develop. Many of the bugs can simply be removed by hand or hosed away with a strong stream of water.

When using chemical pesticides, be very careful, and follow the label instructions to the letter. Spray or dust only those plants to be treated, not any other areas. And when possible, choose pesticides that work on your specific problem.

Sprayers

Sprayers will effectively combat a wide variety of lawn and garden pests. They are used for applying liquid pesticides, whereas dusters are used for applying dry pesticides. The chemical pesticides or herbicides that are used in sprayers either come in liquid form, in water-soluble form, or as wettable powders. Wettable powders do not dissolve; they are kept suspended in the water while being sprayed on the plants.

The chemical concentrate is always mixed in the sprayer's container, according to the manufacturer's specifications detailed on the label. Follow these specifications carefully. Don't assume that if the recommended amount is good, more is even better.

Selection. To determine which type of sprayer to buy, consider the advantages and disadvantages of each. **Hose-end** sprayers don't require pumping, and while their range is limited by the hose length, they put out a large volume quickly, which you'll want for lawns or massed shrubs. **Compression** sprayers generally have a 2 to 3-gallon capacity, can go anywhere and are more precise, but they are somewhat more likely to get clogged. It's best to keep to the sprayer with a 2-gallon capacity; larger compression sprayers are very heavy when full, which makes them difficult to carry around. **Slide-type** (trombone) sprayers can produce the farthest-reaching stream, but they require continual pumping and the stream is not constant.

All sprayers, whatever their type, have two problems: (1) their metal parts tend to corrode unless kept clean and (2) the nozzles can clog up easily.

Materials. Sprayers tend to be made of a material that's highly resistant to corrosion, such as brass, stainless or galvanized steel, or plastic. Regardless of the material, all sprayers should be thoroughly cleaned after use or the chemicals will eventually cause problems and erode the material.

Fittings on sprayers used to be made of either brass or galvanized steel, but high-impact plastic is now used widely, even in the best equipment, since it is less prone to corrosion or rust.

Nozzles. The nozzle is most subject to being plugged by small particles of grass or dirt. It should be easily removable for cleaning. Two types are commonly used in home gardening: (1) the hollow-cone nozzle and (2) the flat-fan nozzle. The hollow-cone nozzle is used to spray pesticides and fungicides on shrubs. It can be adjusted from a thin stream to a fine mist. A flat-fan nozzle is best for applying herbicides; it gives more precision and control.

Tanks. The sprayer tank should have a wide mouth for convenient filling. Many have a funnel-shape top, which directs any chemicals or water that may spill around the edges during filling to run down into the tank rather than down the sides. The wide top also makes it easier to rinse and drain the sprayer and to thoroughly wash out any particles of debris in the tank that can clog the hose.

Also look for a good, solid base. This will keep the sprayer from tipping over while you are pumping air into it.

Valves and Hoses. Some of the new compression sprayers have safety valves that automatically open when the pressure reaches a sufficient level. These valves can also be used to release the pressure in the tank when you're finished spraying. This is a more convenient way to release pressure than by unscrewing the top.

The hoses should be of two or three-ply reinforced rubber or vinyl to resist cracking.

There should be at least one filter (usually located at the base of the wand) that can be quickly removed and cleaned when necessary.

Spray Nozzles

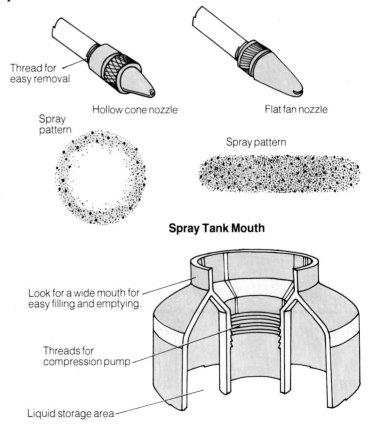

Thread for easy removal

Hollow cone nozzle

Flat fan nozzle

Spray pattern

Spray pattern

Spray Tank Mouth

Look for a wide mouth for easy filling and emptying.

Threads for compression pump

Liquid storage area

Types of Sprayers

Hose-End Sprayer

A hose-end sprayer is a glass or plastic jar suspended beneath a nozzle that attaches to the end of a hose. The jar contains the spray concentrate, and the nozzle will mix that concentrate with the stream of water in a precise amount.

Mixing Ratios. Most hose-ends have a fixed mixing ratio built into the nozzle. This ratio can vary from 5:1 (5 parts water to 1 part concentrate) to 14:1. Because this ratio (as well as the mixing ratio called for on the chemical bottle) can cause some confusion for first-time users, here is an example of how it works.

Let's say that the directions on the chemical you are mixing call for 1 tablespoon of chemical to 1 gallon of water and that your hose-end has a fixed mixing ratio of 14:1. First put 14 tablespoons of chemical in the jar, and then add enough water to raise the contents to the 1-gallon mark on the side of the jar. The hose-end mixes this concentrate with the water so that it comes out at 1 tablespoon of chemical to every gallon of water going through the hose. What you do is take the amount of chemical the directions call for per gallon of water and multiply by the first number in the mixing ratio (5 if the ratio is 5:1, or 14 if the ratio is 14:1).

Some hose-ends are adjustable, in which case you don't have to premix. A dial on the top has up to 16 different settings for whatever dilution you desire. The blending and dilution is all done in the spraying head. Just pour the chemical in the jar; the sprayer takes care of the rest. This type also saves you money, since there is no leftover mixture to throw away —you can pour the unused portion of undiluted chemical back into its original container. There are also hose-end nozzle heads that attach directly to the original chemical bottle. This is the simplest system of all. When you're finished, just clean out the nozzle head.

Hose-end sprayers have adjustable nozzles for covering a wide area with a mist, a fan-shape spray, or a straight stream (for reaching tree tops). The nozzles can also be adjusted to direct the spray up against the underside of plant leaves.

Compression Sprayers

The versatility of these sprayers makes them about the most widely used type in the country. They are relatively light and portable, and their wands and adjustable nozzles make application precise. You can buy 1-pint up to 1-gallon capacity sprayers for the greenhouse or potted plants or

Hose-End Sprayer

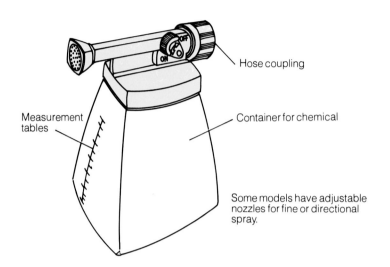

Hose coupling

Measurement tables

Container for chemical

Some models have adjustable nozzles for fine or directional spray.

Compression Sprayers

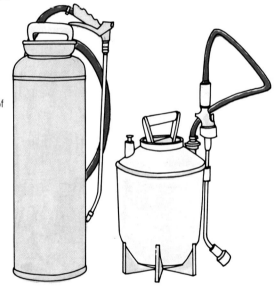

Sprayers are made of metal or plastic and come in sizes from 1 to 4 gallons.

Using a Compression Sprayer

1. Mix chemical and water to the recommended proportions directly in tank or first in a plastic container and then pour mix into tank.

2. Place the pump assembly back in and tighten. Pump up until pressure makes pumping very difficult.

3. Use the spray nozzle to apply chemicals to your lawn or plants.

2 up to 4-gallon sizes for general lawn and garden work.

To operate these sprayers, first add the proper proportions of chemical and water to the tank, and secure the top. Then, with a handle, pump air into the tank until pressure builds up. When you're ready to apply the pesticide, press the trigger. This opens a valve at the end of the hose, and the compressed air forces the liquid spray out the nozzle.

The nozzle can be adjusted to deliver a fine mist for dense, low-growing plants. Larger models emit a 15 to 30-foot stream to reach tree tops. The size of the wand varies according to the size of the entire unit, but most are long enough so that you can spray close to the ground or the underside of leaves without having to bend over.

The *larger compressed-air sprayers* range in size from a 1 to a 4-gallon capacity. The actual liquid capacity is always slightly less to allow room for the compressed air.

These sprayers usually require you to pump up the pressure twice in order to empty the tank. The pump handle may also function as the carrying handle. Larger tanks usually have a strap for carrying the unit over one shoulder.

For relatively small jobs around the greenhouse or garden, the *quart-size compressed-air sprayer* is convenient. The spraying head is mounted on a plastic container that unscrews to be filled or cleaned. A plunger on the spraying head is pumped to force air into the container.

The short spraying wand is attached directly to the head. The nozzle can be adjusted from a fine mist to a direct stream.

Pump Sprayers

For large jobs that require you to do extensive walking, the *backpack pump sprayer* is worth considering. Made of high-impact plastic or galvanized steel, this type handles up to 5 gallons of spray mix. The displacement pump is operated by constantly working a lever with one hand while directing the spray with the other.

The pump handle is also linked to an agitator in the tank, which keeps wettable powders in suspension and prevents them from settling to the bottom.

The nozzle can be adjusted from a fine mist to a standard spray to a 40-foot stream.

Although backpack pump sprayers are contoured to fit your back and equipped with padded, adjustable shoulder straps, you need strength to carry them around. The container alone weighs 8 to 15 pounds, and water adds about another 8 pounds per gallon. However, the heaviness of the pack is offset by your ability to go longer

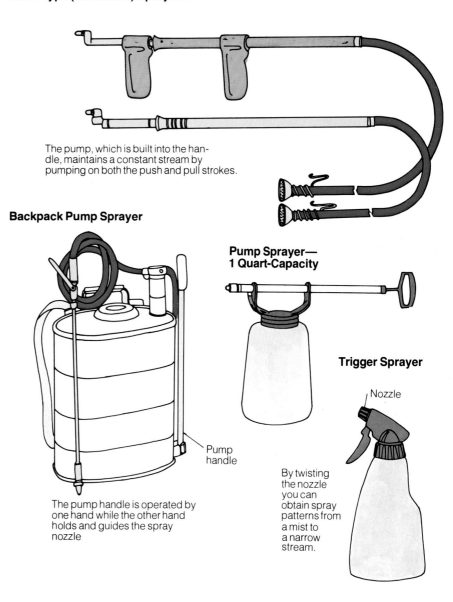

Slide-Type (Trombone) Sprayers

The pump, which is built into the handle, maintains a constant stream by pumping on both the push and pull strokes.

Backpack Pump Sprayer

The pump handle is operated by one hand while the other hand holds and guides the spray nozzle

Pump handle

Pump Sprayer— 1 Quart-Capacity

Trigger Sprayer

Nozzle

By twisting the nozzle you can obtain spray patterns from a mist to a narrow stream.

between refills (since it contains a lot of solution) and by the relative ease of carrying a 40-pound pack on your back rather than a 25-pound sprayer over one shoulder.

Slide-Type Sprayers

These trombone-action sprayers are pumps, not compression sprayers. The pump, which is built into the handle, has an action that works on both the push and pull strokes to maintain a constant stream.

This type of sprayer throws the spray further than any other type of hand-operated sprayer, which makes it quite effective for spraying fruit trees. It is best suited for high-pressure spraying jobs around the home where you don't have to keep

moving the bucket.

Application is simple: You premix the solution and place it in a bucket, then drop the end of the trombone hose into the bucket. The hoses are about 6 feet long and the end in the bucket has a filter screen. The hose has a clip or a heavily weighted end to keep it from pulling out of the bucket. The pumping action (provided by you) sucks the spray out; you then direct it.

The nozzle rotates up or down for spraying the undersides of leaves and adjusts from a spray to a stream reaching 25 feet or more. Wand extensions of up to 9 inches are available for greater reach.

The *1-quart-capacity brass slide* pump and nozzle is a powerful but compact spray gun that's mounted on a plastic bottle. The nozzle adjusts from a spray to a stream. These are excellent for spraying roses and other flowers near the house.

For small jobs around the house or patio, use the *trigger sprayer*—a simple plastic squeeze-pump mounted on a plastic bottle. Commonly used as misters, this inexpensive sprayer also works well for applying pesticides to outdoor plants. If you use it for pesticides, though, be sure to mark the bottle clearly and to use it only for that purpose. (Use another bottle for misting with water.)

Safety Tips

Use common sense when using pesticides. Work on calm days; if there is a slight breeze, spray with the wind at your back, and back away from what you have sprayed. If your skin tends to be sensitive, wear long sleeves and gloves when working with the chemicals. Rubber kitchen gloves or disposable plastic gloves will repell spilled liquid chemicals without hampering your dexterity.

Dust masks and respirators offer protection against the inhalation of chemical spray or dust. If the chemical is blown back over you, the masks and respirators don't block it completely, but they do screen out most of it. They generally are only necessary when you're working on trees, where the spray goes up and then settles down around you.

When you are spraying both pesticides and herbicides, if possible don't use one sprayer for both functions. Use two different sprayers, and mark each one clearly. If you do use only one sprayer, take extra care to clean it thoroughly after using it.

Maintenance

Keep your sprayer clean or corrosion will result. After spraying, unscrew the nozzle and check to make sure it isn't clogged. Empty the container, and dispose of any leftover chemical according to the directions on the pesticide label. Then thoroughly rinse out the container three times. During the last rinsing, put the top on the sprayer and run water through the hose and/or nozzle.

Apply oil to moving parts as required; follow the directions on your particular sprayer. The gaskets on pumps are usually made of neoprene rubber or leather and need an occasional oiling.

Nozzles often have a small filter that should be cleaned regularly. This is especially important when toxic materials have been used.

Hang the sprayer upside down when it's not in use so that it can drain and dry completely.

Trouble-Shooting a Compression Sprayer
(Illustrations are keyed to text at right.)

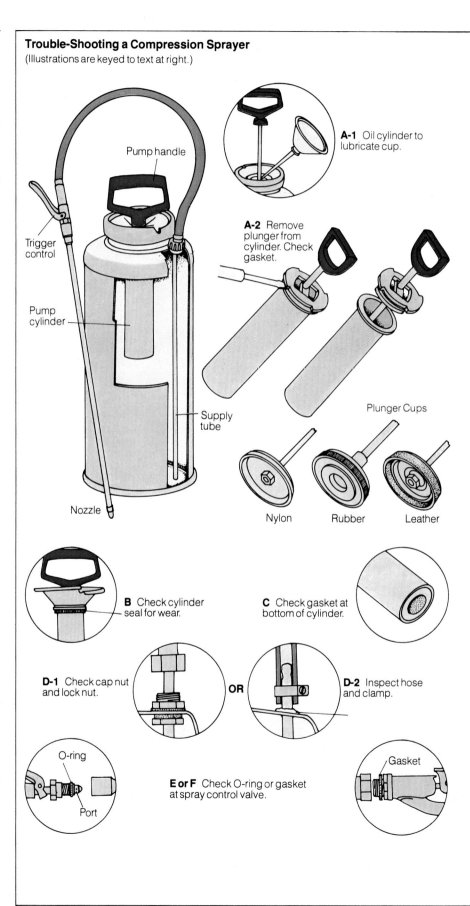

Pump handle

Trigger control

Pump cylinder

Nozzle

Supply tube

A-1 Oil cylinder to lubricate cup.

A-2 Remove plunger from cylinder. Check gasket.

Plunger Cups

Nylon   Rubber   Leather

B Check cylinder seal for wear.

C Check gasket at bottom of cylinder.

D-1 Check cap nut and lock nut.

OR

D-2 Inspect hose and clamp.

O-ring

Port

E or F Check O-ring or gasket at spray control valve.

Gasket

Compression Sprayer Trouble-Shooting Guide

If your sprayer is not working properly, check the following list to analyze the problem. Then follow the steps in the order they are given. Try the second step only if the first one does not work.

A. Problem: Sprayer does not pump up. No resistance when pumping. **Analysis:** Plunger cup is not in contact with cylinder walls.
1. Squirt a tablespoon of oil in top of cylinder to lubricate cup.
2. Pry handle from cylinder. Check cup at bottom. If it's leather, rub oil into it until it's pliable. If it's nylon or rubber, check for wear. If necessary, replace with new cup.

B. Problem: Air hisses out from top of tank when pumped up. Does not hold pressure. **Analysis:** The cylinder seal is dirty or worn.
1. Clean cylinder seal and reseal.
2. Replace seal.

C. Problem: Liquid from tank fills cylinder and wells out of hole in top. **Analysis:** Gasket at bottom of cylinder is dirty or worn.
1. Clean gasket.
2. Replace gasket.

D. Problem: Air leaks from hose connection to tank. **Analysis:** Connection isn't secure. Depending on sprayer:
1. Be sure cap nut and lock nut are threaded down tightly. If that doesn't help, release pressure, remove cap nut, and pull out supply tube. Remove lock nut. Remove inside fitting from tank through pump opening. Remove O-ring and clean surfaces where O-ring seals. If necessary, replace O-ring. Or . . .
2. Inspect hose and clamp. Tighten or replace clamp. Check hose for splits. Cut off worn area and refit hose on tank.

E. Problem: Does not spray when pumped up. **Analysis:** Spray wand is plugged up.
1. Unscrew nozzle. Clean with round toothpick or copper (not steel) wire. Do NOT place to lips to blow out.
2. Clean holes in ends of wand.
3. Clean port at spray control valve.

F. Problem: Spray does not shut off cleanly. **Analysis:** Air is in the line.
1. Refill sprayer if it's empty. Keep tank in upright position. Do not agitate while spraying.
2. Clean and, if necessary, replace O-ring or gasket at spray control valve.

G. Problem: Sprayer does not shut off at all when handle is released. **Analysis:** "Constant-On" latch is engaged or wand is loose.
1. Release "constant-on" latch.
2. Tighten wand at end of spray control valve.

H. Problem: Spray pattern is uneven. **Analysis:** Nozzle is dirty or plugged.
1. Clean nozzle as in E above.
2. Replace nozzle.

Some gardeners prefer dusters to sprayers because they eliminate the need for mixing chemicals. All you do is pour the dry pesticide or fungicide into the container and start pumping. There is also less waste, since you can return the unused powder to its original container instead of throwing it away. However, because the dust can travel only a relatively short distance and is easily blown off course by the slightest breeze, dusters are useful primarily in small gardens or greenhouses.

Good dusters work on each stroke of the pump to maintain a constant fine cloud of material. Choose one with a nozzle that adjusts up or down; this will make it easier to coat the underside of leaves.

Hand pumps are all essentially the same. The difference is largely in how much pesticide they will hold. The smaller ones, which hold only about 4 ounces, are good for spot applications in small areas. Larger hand pumps hold about 1 pound of dusting material. Extension wands of up to 20 inches will give you precise application control and keep the pesticide away from you.

For really big jobs, use the **crank duster**. This is made of epoxy-coated galvanized steel and will hold about 8 pounds of average-weight dust. It can be used for crop dusting or for mosquito control. The cranking action does three things at once: (1) it keeps the dust agitated in the hopper, (2) it premixes the dust with air in the mixing tube, and (3) it turns a high-speed fan to deliver the dust.

Attachments for the crank duster include either a straight tube that makes it possible to work close to the ground without stooping excessively or a flexible Y-tube for covering two rows at a time.

Maintenance
Keep dusters clean. Tap them to remove all the material that remains in the cracks and clings to surfaces. Lubricate with graphite, not oil—the powdered materials will stick to oil.

Dusters

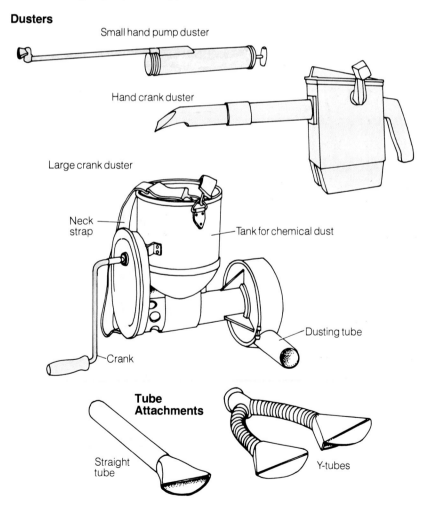

Small hand pump duster

Hand crank duster

Large crank duster

Neck strap

Tank for chemical dust

Crank

Dusting tube

Tube Attachments

Straight tube

Y-tubes

MAINTAINING YOUR POWER EQUIPMENT

Save your money and needless trips to the repair shop—this chapter shows you how to maintain your own power tools. Learn the simple basics of small engines, how to trouble-shoot and do routine tune-ups. Enjoy the satisfaction of doing it yourself.

Even if you give your hand tools expert care, you may be hesitant to work on your power equipment. You can dispel some of the mystery of power equipment by learning the basics of small-engine operation, as discussed in this section.

When in doubt as to whether your machinery requires professional attention, consult your owner's manual and the section in this book called "When to Take Your Engine to a Repair Shop," page 95.

Cleaning
All power equipment, whether electrical or gasoline, should be wiped with a clean rag after each use. Pay particular attention to the cooling fins on gasoline engines where grass clippings tend to get trapped. Always clean carefully around the openings for gasoline and oil so that when the caps are removed debris won't fall into the tanks.

Sharpening
Actually, not many power tools need sharpening, aside from lawn mowers. For specific instructions, see pages 26 and 40. Sharpening a reel mower will not be covered here. However, sharpening a rotary blade is a relatively simple operation, and you'll probably decide to do the job yourself.

Lubricating
Whenever metal moves against metal, it needs to be kept lubricated—oiled or greased—so that the parts can move freely. Lubrication prevents engine wear, so if you want your engine to last you must keep to a very strict lubrication schedule.

◀

This mower looks straightforward enough. It is. Maintain it yourself!

All your garden equipment, whether powered by gas or electricity, requires lubrication. Engine oil lubricates the internal parts; other oils help keep external surfaces and parts rust-free and operating smoothly. Grease is oil that is thickened with a special soap; it is used to lubricate moving parts that run at high temperatures. Your owner's manual gives detailed instructions for lubricating your particular piece of equipment. Many types of grease are available, but "general-purpose" grease is what most types of garden equipment require.

Since grease attracts and holds dirt, use it primarily in areas where it will be covered—for example, inside the wheel housing on lawn mowers, rotary tillers, and garden tractors. Check your owner's manual for information on specific points

Lubricating Tools

that need to be greased as well as frequency of application.

Grease Fittings: Larger pieces of equipment have several grease fittings at different locations on the machine (see your owner's manual to find out where). These fittings are small, nipplelike projections, all of a standard size. Fit the tip of the grease gun over them; then pump grease into that area to lubricate the moving parts. Wipe the nipples clean before and after applying the grease, or else you may shoot dirt and grit into the machinery.

Lubricating Tools: Even if the only moving-parts tool you own is a lawn mower, you need the basic items illustrated below to keep it lubricated, rust-free, and working smoothly.

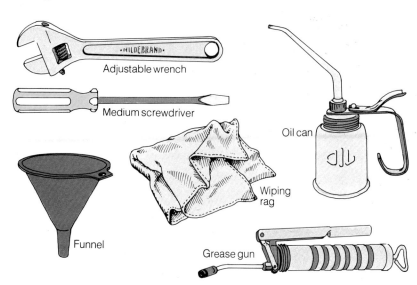

Adjustable wrench

Medium screwdriver

Oil can

Wiping rag

Funnel

Grease gun

ELECTRICAL EQUIPMENT

Several power tools come with electrical motors, including hedge clippers, chainsaws, rotary mowers, nylon string trimmers, and edgers.

The amperage ("amps") the motor needs to run is a measure of the strength of current needed to make the tool do its intended job. Therefore, the more amps that are needed, the more powerful the motor will be. Amps also can be converted into horsepower, the more familiar measure of current or machine strength. Thus, 10 amps are equal to ½ horsepower, 16 amps to 1 horsepower, and 24 amps to 2 horsepower. Most electrical garden equipment falls within the 10- to 24-amp range. Read the label on the motor to find out the strength of your equipment.

The motor housing—the protective covering around the motor—is another consideration. A metal housing requires a three-prong plug. If a short should ever occur in the wiring, this third wire will prevent the current from traveling through the metal housing and shocking the user. Motors with plastic housing require only a two-prong plug. Better-quality motors also have roller bearings at either end of the rotating shaft (called the armature); lesser-quality motors have bushings.

To prevent the trigger switch from burning out, don't stop the motor while you're in the midst of heavy work. The current that flows across the contact points when you activate the motor (via the trigger switch) may not stop immediately; it could arc across the contacts and damage them. Therefore, let the motor idle a moment before releasing the trigger switch.

Start the motor and let it reach full speed before actually using the equipment. In fact, it's better for the motor to operate at close to full speed than at a slow speed.

Maintenance

Keep electrical motors free of water and dust or dirt. With a light oil, lubricate the motor only as often as the instructions suggest—too much oil could cause damage. In addition, make sure that there is absolutely no water in the area where you are operating the equipment—the combination of water and electricity is dangerous. Never drag electrical cords through puddles or plug them in with wet hands.

You should be aware that choosing cords for electrical garden equipment is not an arbitrary decision. First, determine the length of cord you think you'll need. Then select the gauge of cord according to both the required length and the amps required by the motor. The following chart will help you make these selections.

Replacing a Plug: The insulation on an electrical appliance cord can become worn or broken, exposing the wires. This situation is both a shock hazard and a fire hazard; it should be corrected immediately. If the insulation is worn in the middle of the cord, wrap that section with several layers of plastic electrician's tape. If it's worn near the plug, cut the cord to eliminate the worn area, and then reinstall the plug.

To reinstall the plug, first remove the old wiring from the plug. Pry up the protective plate around the two prongs to expose the terminal screws. Loosen them and remove the old wire.

Push the good section of wire through the plug hole, and split the cord back about 3 inches. Strip about 1 inch of insulation from the ends. Tie the cord in the underwriter's knot (see illustration), then pull the knot firmly against the plug.

Twist the strands of each wire into a rope. Then wrap each one, clockwise, under a terminal screw. Make the wrap two-thirds to three-quarters around. Tighten the screws and replace the cover plate.

Changing Brushes on Electrical Motors: Worn brushes may cause an electrical power tool to run poorly or even fail to run. Brushes are actually carbon blocks that press against the armature (often called a rotor) in the motor. They conduct electricity and are instrumental in setting up the electromagnetic field that makes the motor turn.

Brushes are usually good for years of service, but they can wear down. If the engine is running poorly or not at all, check the brushes. They normally are located under a slotted cap that unscrews from the motor housing. When removing the cap, be careful that the brushes don't fly out—they are spring loaded.

If the brushes are worn thinner than they are wide, replace them. Make sure the spring is firm enough to provide good pressure. If the brushes are in good shape and the motor still runs poorly, the problem may be a dirty armature. Remove the motor housing and spray the armature with electrical contact cleaner (often sold as a TV-tuner cleaner).

Replacing a Plug

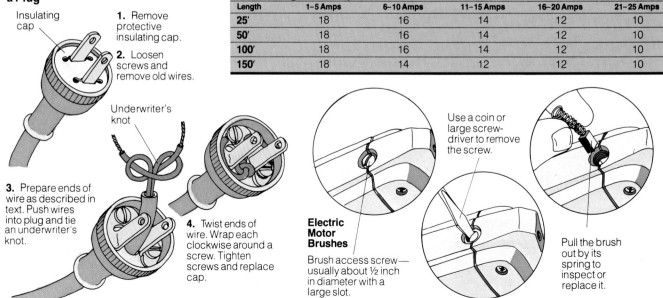

1. Remove protective insulating cap.

2. Loosen screws and remove old wires.

3. Prepare ends of wire as described in text. Push wires into plug and tie an underwriter's knot.

4. Twist ends of wire. Wrap each clockwise around a screw. Tighten screws and replace cap.

Insulating cap

Underwriter's knot

Electric Motor Brushes

Brush access screw—usually about ½ inch in diameter with a large slot.

Use a coin or large screwdriver to remove the screw.

Pull the brush out by its spring to inspect or replace it.

Wire Gauge for Amp Load					
Length	1–5 Amps	6–10 Amps	11–15 Amps	16–20 Amps	21–25 Amps
25′	18	16	14	12	10
50′	18	16	14	12	10
100′	18	16	14	12	10
150′	18	14	12	12	10

GASOLINE-POWERED EQUIPMENT

The two types of small gasoline engines most commonly found in gardeners' tool storage areas are: (1) the four-cycle engine (used on lawn mowers, rotary tillers, and other large equipment) and (2) the two-cycle engine (used on chainsaws, gas-powered blowers, and weed cutters). The "cycles" refer to how the engine is powered: in the four-cycle engine, power is produced during one of every four strokes of the piston; in the two-cycle engine, power is produced on every downstroke. The other major difference between the two engines is the fuel system. In the four-cycle engine, the oil and gas are kept separate; in the two-cycle engine, they are mixed together. However, both types of engines operate on the same basic principles, which are outlined below.

Both two-cycle and four-cycle engines are cooled by air rather than by water and they usually have only one piston (although some four-cycle engines have two). Some equipment comes with a battery and a starting mechanism, but most small engines are started by pulling a rope. This action turns the engine over—that is, the piston goes up and down and sets a whole chain of events in motion.

Ignition

As the engine begins turning over, the flywheel moves. Attached to one point of the flywheel are one or more magnets. These pass very close to a coil mounted inside the engine, creating a magnetic force.

Parts of a Small Gasoline Engine

When you pull the starter rope, you "turn the engine over," setting in motion a whole chain of events.

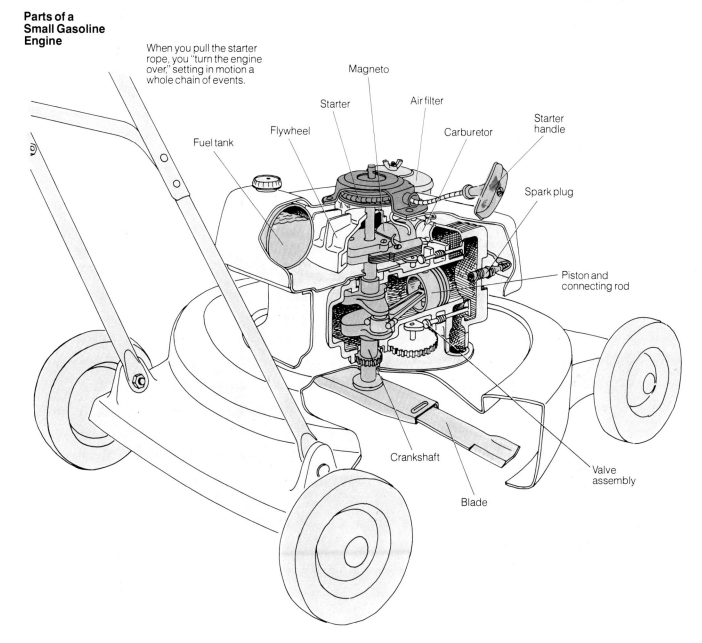

Magneto · Starter · Air filter · Flywheel · Carburetor · Starter handle · Fuel tank · Spark plug · Piston and connecting rod · Crankshaft · Valve assembly · Blade

Note: This drawing and others in this section show the fundamentals of engine operation and generally how to maintain them. Since all engines vary in design, the relative positions of some parts may not be the same as on your particular engine. For the specifics on any engine, write to the manufacturer for their Maintenance or Repair Manual, which is not the same as the Owner's Manual and does not usually come with a new piece of equipment.

Within the coil there are two sets of copper wire windings: (1) a thick, inner "primary" wire, which has about 100–200 turns, and (2) a thin, outer "secondary" wire, which has about 10–20,000 turns. The primary wire leads to a set of breaker points and to a condenser. The secondary wire leads to the spark plug.

When the starter rope is pulled, it moves the crankshaft, which has a teardrop-shape lobe or a flat spot on it. This cam on the crankshaft opens and closes the breaker points. When the points are closed, the electrical current, set up by the turning flywheel passing near the coil, flows through the primary wire. However, just before a spark is needed, the breaker points are opened, breaking the circuit of the current in the primary wire, causing the magnetic field to reverse and collapse. This creates a very high voltage which is picked up by the thin secondary wire. The condenser absorbs the current in the *primary* current so that it does not jump the gap in the breaker points. The high-voltage *secondary* current is then channeled through the thin secondary wire and the spark plug wire to the spark plug center electrode. The unstable current seeks a ground, and as it jumps to the spark plug's ground electrode, it causes a spark.

This electrical process is repeated with each revolution of the flywheel. The faster the flywheel turns, the faster the spark is ignited in the combustion chamber, and the more fuel is required to keep up this speed.

Compression

As the engine begins turning over with the pull of the starter rope, air is sucked through the air filter, down an air horn, and through the carburetor. At the same time, gasoline is drawn into the carburetor from the fuel tank. The air and fuel are mixed very precisely by the carburetor as they are drawn into the combustion chamber between the spark plug and the top of the piston.

At this point, the spark leaps across the gap on the spark plug electrodes and ignites the mixture of fuel and air in the combustion chamber. The mixture explodes, creating a force that drives the piston down.

The piston is linked by the connecting rod to the crankshaft (the driving mechanism of the engine), which is turned by the up-and-down motion of the piston.

The rotating crankshaft is linked to the "business end" of the power equipment (e.g., the blade on a lawn mower or the chain on a saw). This link can either be direct (i.e., the equipment is attached right to the shaft) or indirect (i.e., the equipment is connected via a belt, chain, or gear).

The Electrical System

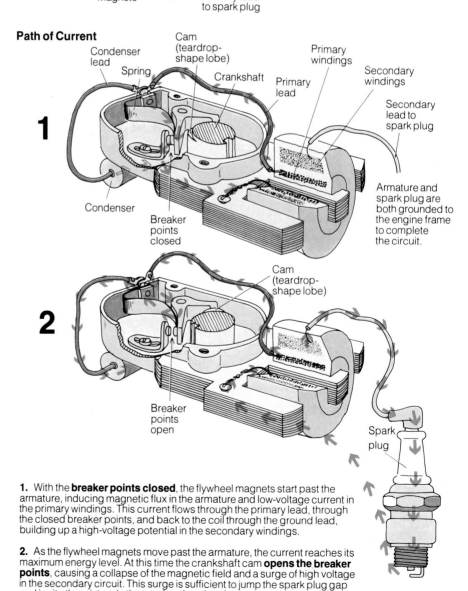

The permanent magnets in the flywheel rim pass the armature and coil to induce an electric current.

Path of Current

1. With the **breaker points closed**, the flywheel magnets start past the armature, inducing magnetic flux in the armature and low-voltage current in the primary windings. This current flows through the primary lead, through the closed breaker points, and back to the coil through the ground lead, building up a high-voltage potential in the secondary windings.

2. As the flywheel magnets move past the armature, the current reaches its maximum energy level. At this time the crankshaft cam **opens the breaker points**, causing a collapse of the magnetic field and a surge of high voltage in the secondary circuit. This surge is sufficient to jump the spark plug gap and ignite the mixture in the combustion chamber.

THE TWO-CYCLE ENGINE

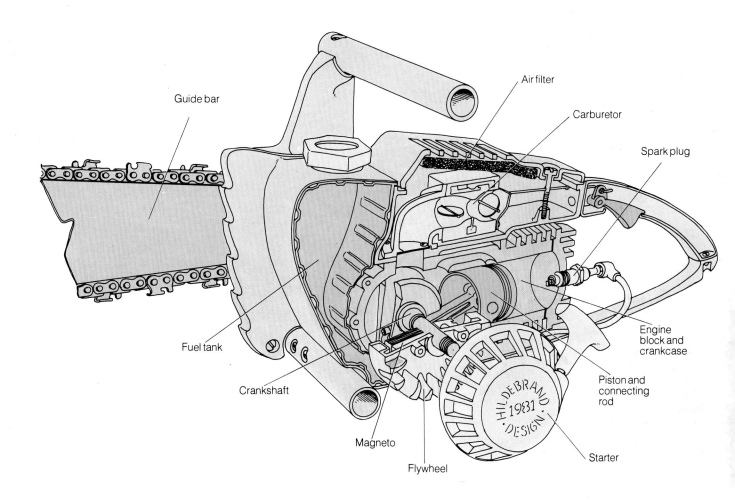

Guide bar

Air filter

Carburetor

Spark plug

Fuel tank

Crankshaft

Magneto

Flywheel

Starter

Engine block and crankcase

Piston and connecting rod

Despite the similar principles behind the operation of the two-cycle and four-cycle engines, each kind has variations. To spot variations in engine design from one piece of equipment to another or from one manufacturer to another, examine your owner's manual and the engine itself.

The illustrations on these pages show typical two-cycle and four-cycle engines on a chainsaw and lawn mower. Use these illustrations and this text to familiarize yourself with the general operating principles. Then you will be able to locate the same systems on your own equipment.

It is in the fuel system that the basic difference between the two engines is found. This system consists of a gas tank, a gas line, and the carburetor where the fuel is mixed with air and pumped into the combustion chamber. There are three types of fuel systems: (1) the gravity-feed system, which is used when the gas tank is

located above the carburetor; (2) the fuel pump, which is used when the gas tank is located below the carburetor; and (3) the diaphragm, or suction feed, system, which is used on equipment that is held at a variety of angles while in operation.

The Two-Cycle Engine

In the two-cycle engine, the fuel mixture is first moved via a diaphragm or suction feed carburetor into a crankcase and then into the combustion chamber. When the piston is initially moved upward by a pull of the starter rope, it changes the pressure in the crankcase, causing a thin rubber diaphragm to pulsate and draw fuel through a valve into the carburetor where it is mixed with air. That same upstroke of the piston also creates a low-pressure area below the piston, drawing the fuel mixture from

the carburetor through a port or tube into the crankcase.

The fuel mixture that is already above the piston is compressed; the spark plug fires and ignites the mixture, which explodes, expands, and drives the piston down. As the piston drops, it exposes the exhaust port, and the spent gases are expelled. Almost at the same moment, the fresh fuel mixture in the crankcase is forced up into the combustion chamber above the piston. As the piston again moves up toward the spark plug, the fuel mix is compressed for the next spark and explosion. Simultaneously, the diaphragm pulsates and again draws fuel into the carburetor and the air-fuel mix from the carburetor into the crankcase.

Since every downstroke of a two-cycle engine is a power stroke, this engine sounds twice as fast as a four-cycle engine running at the same speed.

The Two-Cycle Engine— Diaphagm Fuel System

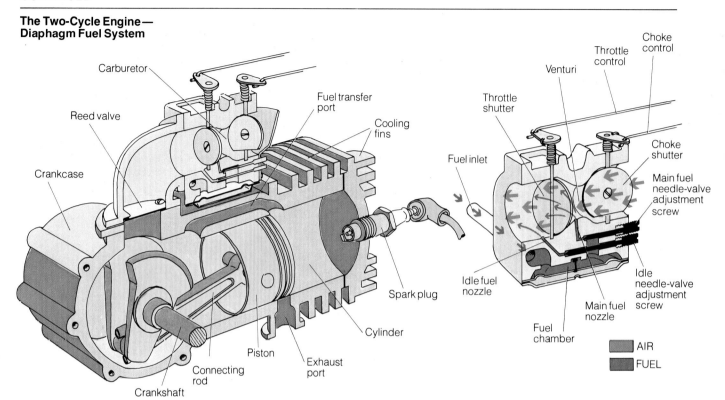

Carburetor
Reed valve
Crankcase
Fuel transfer port
Cooling fins
Spark plug
Cylinder
Piston
Exhaust port
Connecting rod
Crankshaft

Choke control
Throttle control
Venturi
Throttle shutter
Fuel inlet
Choke shutter
Main fuel needle-valve adjustment screw
Idle fuel nozzle
Main fuel nozzle
Fuel chamber
Idle needle-valve adjustment screw

AIR
FUEL

How the Two-Cycle Engine Operates

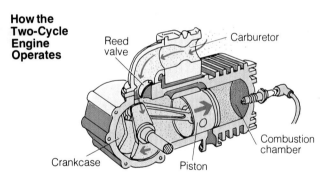

Reed valve
Carburetor
Crankcase
Piston
Combustion chamber

1. When the piston moves toward the spark plug, the lower pressure opens the reed valve and sucks fuel mixture into the crankcase from the carburetor. At the same time, the fuel mixture already in the combustion chamber is compressed.

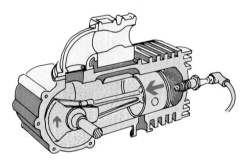

2. When the piston is at the "top" of its stroke, the spark plug fires and ignites the compressed fuel mixture. The explosion drives the piston back toward the crankcase, producing the engine's power by turning the crankshaft.

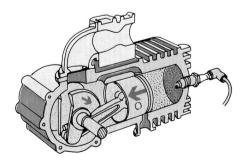

3. As the piston slides along the cylinder, it compresses the fuel in the crankcase, closing the reed valve.

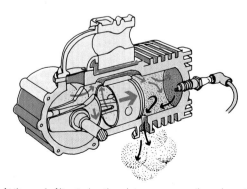

4. At the end of its stroke, the piston uncovers the exhaust port and the transfer port. The compressed fuel mixture in the crankcase expands into the combustion chamber, forcing the spent gases out of the exhaust port.

THE FOUR-CYCLE ENGINE

The four-cycle engine is similar to the two-cycle except that the fuel is drawn directly from the carburetor into the combustion chamber, and out of every four strokes the piston makes (two up and two down), only one of them produces power.

The fuel mixture in a four-cycle engine is moved either by a gravity-feed carburetor or by a fuel pump. However, the fuel pump system is rarely found in the type of equipment discussed in this book. The gravity-feed system is most common; it is used in equipment where the fuel tank is located above the carburetor.

The float carburetor is a typical gravity-feed carburetor found on four-cycle engines. Here, fuel flows into a bowl in the carburetor containing a float mechanism (similar to the kind used in a toilet to maintain the water level). When the fuel level drops as it flows out to the engine, the float also drops and opens a valve that allows more fuel to flow into the bowl. As the level of gasoline increases, the float rises and shuts the valve. This system keeps a constant supply of gasoline ready to be drawn into the carburetor.

When the piston first starts down, by the pull of the starting rope, a valve opens in the combustion chamber above the piston. The downward motion creates a low-pressure area that draws a mixture of gas and air directly from the carburetor through a valve and into the combustion chamber.

The piston then rises, compressing the fuel-air mixture, and the intake valve closes.

Just before the piston is ready to go down again, the spark plug ignites the compressed fuel-air mixture, which explodes, expands, and drives the piston down, just as in the two-cycle engine.

On the fourth and last stroke of the series, the piston rises, the exhaust valve

The Four-Cycle Engine (Lawnmower)*

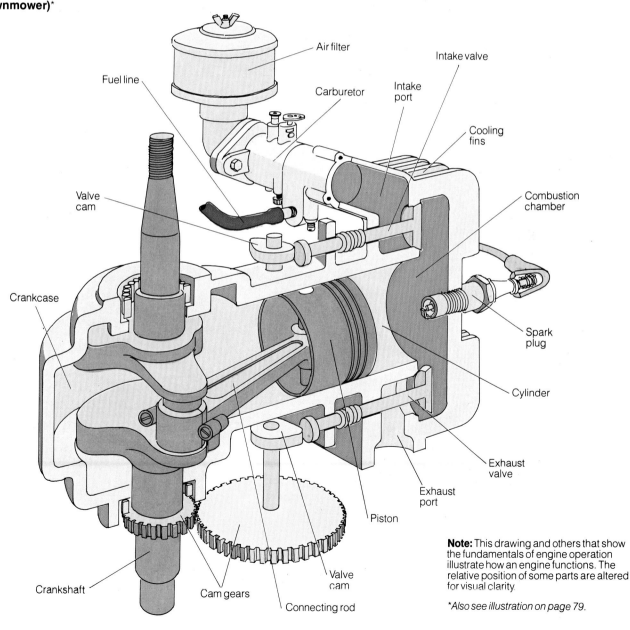

Note: This drawing and others that show the fundamentals of engine operation illustrate how an engine functions. The relative position of some parts are altered for visual clarity.

*Also see illustration on page 79.

**The Four-Cycle Engine—
Float Carburetor Fuel System**

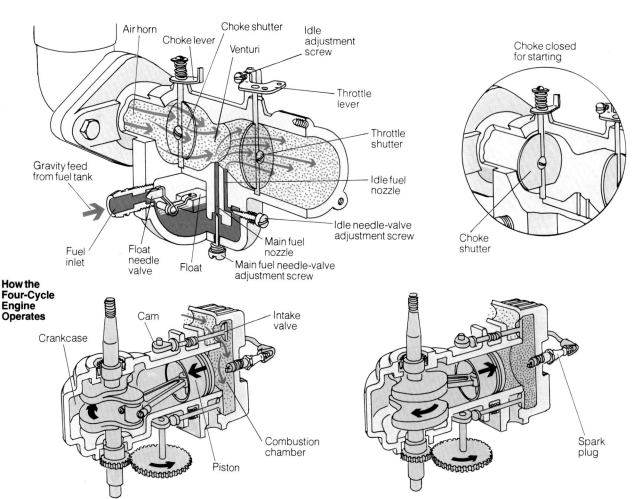

**How the
Four-Cycle
Engine
Operates**

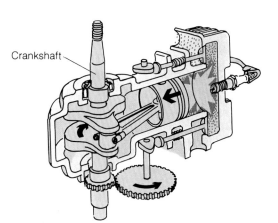

1. On the first stroke the cam opens the intake valve at the same time the piston moves toward the crankcase and sucks fuel mixture into the combustion chamber.

2. The piston moves back toward the spark plug on its second stroke and, with both valves closed, compresses the fuel mixture.

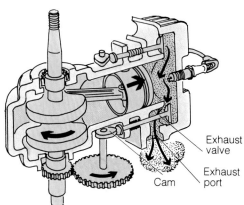

3. At the "top" of the second stroke, the spark plug fires, ignites the fuel mixture, and the resulting explosion drives the piston back for its third stroke, producing the power that turns the crankshaft.

4. As the piston rebounds for its fourth stroke, the exhaust valve opens and the spent gases are pushed out of the exhaust port.

in the combustion chamber opens, and the piston forces out the burned gases.

The Choke

Whether the carburetor functions properly has much to do with the choke. The choke is the thin metal disc that fits in the air horn and controls the air-to-fuel ratio. Closing the choke reduces the amount of air to be mixed with the fuel, thus making the fuel mixture richer. Opening the choke admits more air, thus making the fuel mixture less concentrated, or "leaner." So close the choke when starting a cold engine—the richer mixture makes it easier to start. Then, when the engine begins to run, open the choke—the leaner fuel mix is required for normal engine performance.

Air Filters

Your engine has one of three types of air filters: (1) an oil-bath air filter, (2) an oil-saturated air filter; or (3) a dry-element air filter. Older engines have oil baths or oil-saturated air filters. The oil bath contains a lubricating oil in its base that the air must pass through before it enters the air horn of the carburetor. The dirt and dust from the air accumulate in the bottom of the oil cup. The oil-saturated air filter forces the air through an oil-saturated foam or wire mesh that traps the dirt.

The dry-element air filter is most common. This dry filter—which can be made of foam, regular paper, or pleated paper—traps dust and debris before the air gets sucked into the carburetor, where it could foul the fuel jets or the engine itself. Air filters usually are above the carburetor, in a fitted metal or plastic housing.

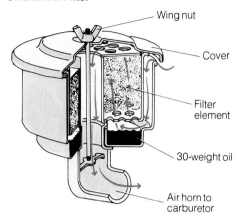

Oil-Bath Air Filter
- Wing nut
- Cover
- Filter element
- 30-weight oil
- Air horn to carburetor

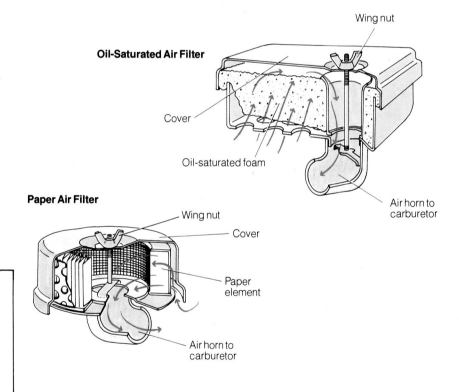

Oil-Saturated Air Filter
- Wing nut
- Cover
- Oil-saturated foam
- Air horn to carburetor

Paper Air Filter
- Wing nut
- Cover
- Paper element
- Air horn to carburetor

FUEL

The same type of gas is used for both two-cycle and four-cycle engines. Use only *fresh*, regular gasoline. Old gasoline does not ignite easily.

How you store fuel is as important as which kind you use. So put the gas in a safety gasoline can, *never* in a glass container.

When you refuel your engine, do it on a driveway or over some dirt, not on the lawn or in your garage. A little fuel almost always gets spilled, and not only is gasoline quite volatile but it also kills the grass on contact. Also, be careful to never refuel a *hot* engine—it can be very dangerous.

You must mix the gas with oil for two-cycle engines. The proportions of gas and oil vary from one piece of equipment to another; see your owner's manual for the exact proportions to use on your machine. Two-cycle oil usually comes in small pint-size cans that are convenient for mixing with one or two gallons of gasoline. To mix

the oil and gas, you can pour the appropriate amount of oil in a gas can and then fill the can with the appropriate amount of gasoline at the pump. If you have more than one two-cycle engine, be sure to keep separate cans for each, labeled and clearly marked with the proper proportions of gas and oil.

Diesel versus Gas

More and more of the larger garden-tractors now have diesel rather than gasoline engines. Diesels are commonly used on large agricultural machinery, and they have many advantages—not the least of which are cheaper fuel and an engine that

will normally outlast a gasoline engine.

Diesel engines do not have spark plugs. Instead, the air and diesel mixture in the combustion chamber is ignited by the sheer pressure of the rising piston. Diesel provides more heat per gallon; gasoline provides more energy per gallon. Not only that, but diesel also saves fuel by mixing with more air. And the absence of a spark plug and a carburetor means that there are fewer parts to go wrong.

Never let a diesel engine run out of fuel, or the fuel lines to the combustion chamber become filled with air. They then must be "bled" (drained) to make room for the fresh diesel fuel.

BASIC TUNE-UP PROCEDURES

Your engine will start promptly and run smoothly each time if you follow these maintenance and tune-up procedures.

Spark Plug

Remove the spark plug after every 50 hours of use or once a year, whichever comes first, and check it for wear. Just looking at the tip of a spark plug can tell you something about your engine's performance and help you decide whether to replace the plug. For example, if the plug is coated with a light brown substance, your engine is probably functioning properly. See "Analyzing Spark Plugs" on the facing page to find out what else to look for and when to install a new plug.

If you have to replace a spark plug, use the size and type recommended by the manufacturer—you must match the original plug or the replacement won't work properly (e.g., a plug that is too long will be mashed by the top of the rising piston). Spark plugs come in many different sizes and lengths, so choose carefully.

Also check the owner's manual to find out what gap is required on the plug. The gap is the space between the side electrode and the center electrode. Its width determines the timing of the spark. New plugs come with preset gaps, but check the gap anyway with an inexpensive spark plug (wire-type) gauge that you can buy at any auto parts store. For example, if the required gap is .025, select that wire on the gauge and slip it between the two electrodes. You know the gap is correct when you feel a slight drag on the gauge. If it is too tight, use the tip of a screwdriver to increase the opening slightly. If it is too loose, tap the side electrode lightly with the wire gauge to tighten the gap.

Parts of a Spark Plug

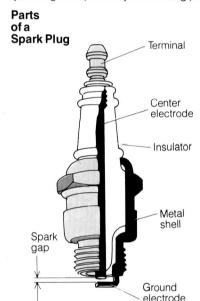

- Terminal
- Center electrode
- Insulator
- Metal shell
- Spark gap
- Ground electrode

Measuring the Spark Plug Gap

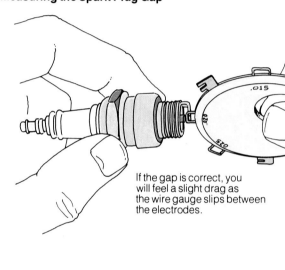

If the gap is correct, you will feel a slight drag as the wire gauge slips between the electrodes.

Adjusting the Spark Plug Gap

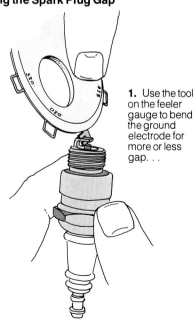

1. Use the tool on the feeler gauge to bend the ground electrode for more or less gap. . .

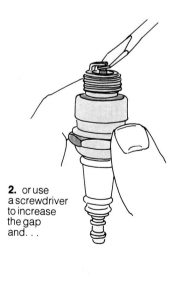

2. or use a screwdriver to increase the gap and. . .

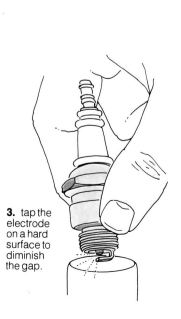

3. tap the electrode on a hard surface to diminish the gap.

Analyzing Spark Plugs

☐ If the spark plug is coated with a light brown deposit, your engine is running properly. Scrape away the deposits with a knife and wire brush, and keep using the same plug. If you can't easily remove the coating because it is too thick, replace the plug.

☐ If the plug on four-cycle engines is black and oily, this usually means that the piston rings are worn and must be replaced—they are allowing oil from the crankcase into the combustion chamber. An oily plug on a two-cycle engine probably indicates too much oil in the oil-gas mixture. Check your owner's manual and correct your mixing procedure.

☐ If the plug is coated with a black powdery deposit, the gas-air mixture is too rich, or else the air filter is clogged. This carbon deposit can cause the plug to ground itself on the engine and spark improperly or not at all. Either clean or replace your air filter.

☐ If the plug is coated with white or yellow deposits, a higher-test gasoline than necessary is being used. Check your manual for the correct type of gasoline to use. These deposits could also mean that there is too much air in the air-fuel mixture. If so, enrich the mixture by adjusting the carburetor: Turn the needle valve counterclockwise very slightly.

☐ If the side electrode is pitted or has a small metallic mound on it, or if the center electrode has a round, worn appearance, this means that the electrodes are burned. Burning can also be indicated by a clean, white look. Burned electrodes are caused by overheating, which can result from any of three causes: (1) an air-fuel mixture that is too lean, (2) clogged cooling fins on the engine, or (3) incorrect engine timing. To correct the air-fuel mixture, adjust the needle valve on the carburetor (see page 92). To clear the cooling fins, simply remove the shroud or cover from the flywheel, and clear the debris (e.g., grass or soil) from the fins with a small stock or probe. To correct the engine timing, check the points to make sure the plug is adjusted to the correct gap (see facing page). To remove the small metallic mound on the side electrode, file between the gap, using a very small file or thin Carborundum paper (special sandpaper with Carborundum as the abrasive). Then reset the points.

☐ A crack on the ceramic end of the plug allows electricity to escape and results in poor engine performance or failure to start. If you see a crack, always replace the plug.

Symptoms and Solutions

Thin, light brown powder
A light brown powdery residue means the engine is running OK...

Remove deposit with a stiff bristle brush.

Black oil
Black, oily deposit means too much oil in the cylinder...

Piston rings

Worn piston rings or (in a two-cycle engine) too much oil in the fuel mix.

Black powder
Black, powdery deposit means too rich a fuel/air mixture...

Air filter

Could be a clogged air filter or running with choke closed.

Yellowish-white deposit
Yellowish or white crusty deposit means too lean an air/fuel mixture, or too much additive in gasoline...

Carburetor

Use lower octane gasoline or adjust needle valves on carburetor.

Needle-valve adjustments

Metallic mound, pitting, or wear
Metallic mound, pitting, or wear means too lean an air/fuel mixture, clogged cooling fins, or incorrect timing...

Use lower octane gasoline or adjust needle valves, clear cooling fins, or check points.

Other symptoms
If engine is running too hot, it may have clogged cooling fins. Clean out grass, mud, and other debris with a small stick.

A cracked spark plug should be replaced as soon as it is detected.

Smooth spark plug electrodes with a piece of Carborundum paper or a small file.

Air Filters

One main reason why engines run poorly or don't start is because the air filter gets clogged, thus reducing the ratio of air to fuel in the carburetor. Therefore, change or clean the filter each time you change the engine oil, or about every 25 operating hours (more if you work where it's dusty). To change or clean any type of air filter, follow these steps:

Oil-Saturated Filter: Loosen the screw that holds the filter housing above the carburetor. Remove the unit and lift off the cover. Remove the foam filter and wash it in kerosene or hot, sudsy water. Squeeze it dry and then saturate it with 30-weight oil. Squeeze lightly to remove excess oil, then replace in filter housing. Make sure lip on top of foam extends over edge of housing so that no dust can get past it. Replace top and remount housing. (See illustration for **oil-bath filter**.)

Pleated Paper Filter: This should be replaced each time it gets dirty, but cleaning will give you an extra season's use. Unscrew the nut on top of the housing and remove the cap and the paper filter. If there is a foam sleeve around the paper filter, slip it off. Tap the filter several times on the sidewalk or on a piece of wood to dislodge dust and debris. If the filter is obviously dirty and tapping doesn't remove much dust, replace it.

Paper Filter: This is less common; it is mounted beside the gas tank and connected to the carburetor by a hose. Remove the hose clamps and hose; then remove the filter. Tap it to clean it. If it's still dirty, replace it.

Cleaning the Oil-Bath Air Filter

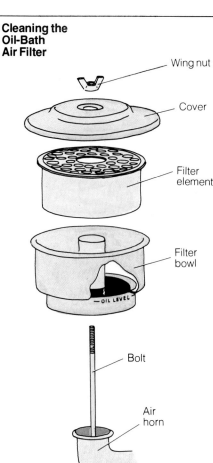

Wing nut

Cover

Filter element

Filter bowl

Bolt

Air horn

1. Remove wing nut and lift off the cover, filter element, and bowl.

2. Rinse the filter element in a solvent, and allow it to drip dry. DO NOT dry it with an air hose.

3. Pour and wipe the dirty oil from the bowl. If there is a lot of sludge in the bottom, you should clean the filter more often.

4. Fill the bottom of the bowl, to the OIL LEVEL line, with 30-weight oil.

5. Replace all the pieces, including any washers or gaskets, in the **same** order you removed them.

Cleaning the Oil-Saturated Air Filter

1. Unscrew wing nut and lift off cover. Remove cup and foam filter element.

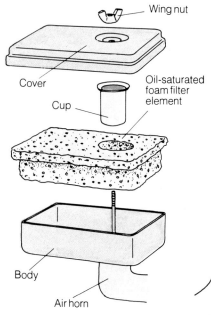

Wing nut

Cover

Cup

Oil-saturated foam filter element

Body

Air horn

Wash foam element in solvent or household detergent and water.

2. Wrap the foam in a towel and squeeze it as dry as possible.

3. Pour new 30-weight motor oil on the foam.

4. Manipulate the foam to distribute the oil evenly and squeeze gently to remove excess.

Changing the Oil

The way to make a four-cycle engine last a long time is to change the oil regularly. Oil that is in too long (usually, more than 25 operating hours) gets dirty, begins to break down, and causes rapid engine-wear (particularly on the piston rings, which hold oil tightly in the cylinder). Then oil begins to leak into the combustion chamber, resulting in poor performance.

It's quite simple to do an oil change. Consult the owner's manual for exact locations of drain and filler plugs for your lawn mower or other equipment. On lawn mowers, the oil drain plug is often under the housing, near the blade, although on some models it may be on the side of the engine, near the bottom.

Spray the engine with water to rinse off dirt, keeping the water off the shroud and fins. Be sure to clean around the opening where the oil is added. Then run the engine for a few minutes—warm oil flows better, and more of the old oil will flow out. Remove the plug with a wrench, and then let the oil drain for at least 10 minutes (20 minutes is better). Replace and tighten the plug.

Now you are ready to put in the new oil. Use the type specified in the owner's manual. If you don't know what type to use, try a good 30-weight oil—it's generally safe. Always use a funnel to prevent spilling oil on the engine or the housing; spilled oil would soon collect dirt and keep the engine from being properly cooled.

Remove the oil filler-plug and pour in the oil. The oil level should be near the bottom of the threads on the filler plug when the plug is tightened down. If the engine has a dip stick, use it—the instructions for your piece of equipment will tell you what oil level to maintain. Do not overfill.

OIL

The weight of oil—its thickness or viscosity—is rated according to a series of numbers printed on top of the can. The cans are marked first with the letters SAE (Society of Automotive Engineers). This is followed by numbers: 10-20, 10-30, 10-40, or just 30. Oil with two sets of numbers normally is used for high-performance car engines. The first number indicates the oil's viscosity when cold; the second indicates the oil's viscosity when hot. If you are operating gardening equipment in sub-freezing weather, change the oil instead of using an oil with a wide-spanning temperature range. Your owner's manual will specify what weight of oil you will need in such cases.

Medium-Service 30-Weight Oil: Unless the equipment manufacturer specifies otherwise, use the medium-service, all-purpose SAE 30 oil for lawn mowers, rotary tillers, garden tractors, and other equipment requiring engine oil. These typically have four-cycle engines in which the oil is not mixed with the gasoline (see page 84).

The weight of the oil is stamped into the top of the can as well as printed on the label.

Two-Cycle Oil is used for engines in which oil and gas are mixed together. It differs from standard oil in that it burns at higher temperatures. This feature makes two-cycle oil more compatible with gasoline.

Transmission Fluid is a special type of lubricant for the automatic transmission found on some rotary tillers, riding lawn mowers, and garden tractors. The transmission fluid must be kept at a certain level in the machine. Read your owner's manual to learn where to add the fluid, how to check its level, and when to change it.

Penetrating Oils are designed primarily to work their way between the threads of stuck nuts and bolts, thus freeing them. These oils also are sprayed on metal tools to prevent rust. Do not use them as a lubricant—they are too light to last.

Changing the Oil

1. Clean the area of the engine around the oil filler plug. Spray with water and then wipe with a rag.

Drain plug

2. Remove the drain plug. Loosen filler plug to counter a partial vacuum.

3. Let the oil drain at least 10 minutes—20 minutes if possible.

Filler plug

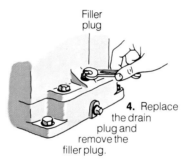

4. Replace the drain plug and remove the filler plug.

5. Pour in the oil using a funnel.

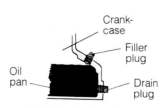

Crank-case
Filler plug
Oil pan
Drain plug

6. To tell when the oil level is right, use the dipstick. If there is no dipstick, fill until the oil level touches the threads of the filler plug.

Breaker Points

Points are the most complex aspect of a basic engine tune-up, but they can be essential. If your engine won't start at all—or if it starts only with difficulty and runs poorly—and you are sure there is no problem with the fuel, ignition system, spark plugs, oil, or air filter, then it's time to check (and possibly replace) the points.

To check and replace the points:

1. Remove the flywheel nut: First, block the flywheel in place. You will need to buy a flywheel holder (see illustration), or you can use a belt.

If you have a Briggs and Stratton engine, chances are that the nut has a left-hand thread, so loosen it with a clockwise pressure. Once the nut is off, you can pull the flywheel.

2. Remove the flywheel: This is easier said than done, since the flywheel is forced on to the tapered end of the crankshaft. Removal is best accomplished with a puller (see illustration), which is commonly found in rental shops. If you don't have a puller, slip a pair of screwdrivers behind the wheel, opposite each other, and begin prying with alternate pulls. Pry in one spot and then turn the flywheel a quarter turn. Tap the flywheel very gently to create vibrations that will

Retaining Key

Crankshaft   Key

key

Flywheel hub

Key slot

When you remove the flywheel, check the fit of the retaining key. It should fit snugly in the slot of the flywheel and the crankshaft (see text).

help loosen it. Keep repeating this process as you work your way around the wheel.

When the flywheel is loosened, check to make sure that the retaining key, which is in a slot between the crankshaft and the flywheel, does not wobble in the slot. If the slot is worn, take the engine to a shop and have the crankshaft replaced. If the key is worn, replace it yourself—but be sure to use a nonferrous key, not an iron or steel one.

Once the flywheel is off, you will see a plate covering the points and condenser. Remove the retaining screws and lift the plate off.

3. Check the points: The points are opened and closed by a lobe attached to the crankshaft (or, in some four-cycle engines, by a separate cam). Turn the crankshaft until the points are as open as

possible. Use a feeler gauge set at the appropriate gap to check this. (Most small engine points are set at .020 inches.) Inspect the points. If they are pitted or if a little metallic hill has built up, replace them. (In an emergency, they can be sanded down for one more day's use.)

When you turn the crankshaft, if the points do not open at all, you may have discovered why the engine won't start. If the points don't open to the proper gap, the engine will run poorly. Usually, when points don't open properly—or don't open at all—it's because the fiber block, which rests against the crankshaft, is worn. If this is the case, you should replace the fiber block. Because the points are mounted on the fiber block and are sold with it as a unit, you'll automatically replace both.

If the fiber block is not worn, check the locking screw that holds the points in place. It may be loose.

4. Replacing and setting points: A set of points has one fixed side and one that is moved in and out by the rotating lobe on the crankshaft. Keep in mind that the fixed point is moved away from the moveable point by an adjusting screw.

To take out the old points, first remove the locking screw. Then remove the wire that connects the coil to the fixed point as well as the wire from the condenser to the moveable point. An exception is the Briggs and Stratton engine, which has only one wire from the condenser to the fixed point.

Put the new points in place and fasten them down lightly with the locking screw. Turn the crankshaft until the tip of the lobe pushes the moveable point away from the fixed point as far as possible. That is the precise gap you need to set.

With the proper feeler gauge (usually .025 or .030) between the points, turn the adjusting screw on the fixed point until you feel a slight drag on the gauge. (On most Briggs and Stratton engines, the adjusting screw moves the condenser, which in turn moves the fixed point.) Check the gap by trying to gently insert the next larger size gauge. It should not slip between the points.

The condenser, which captures extra high-voltage electricity, is normally held in a retaining clip next to the points. Attach the wire from the condenser to the moveable point and the wire from the coil to the fixed point. Again, the exception is the Briggs and Stratton engine where the condenser wire attaches to the fixed point.

Before replacing the points' cover and the flywheel, put a small dab of grease on the crankshaft to reduce wear on the fiber block. The grease often comes in the package with the points.

Removing the Flywheel

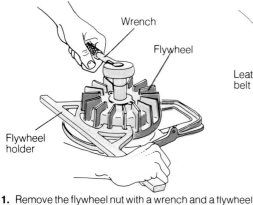

Wrench

Flywheel

Flywheel holder

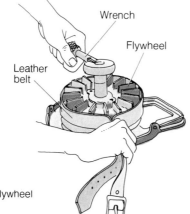

Wrench

Flywheel

Leather belt

1. Remove the flywheel nut with a wrench and a flywheel holder or a leather belt.

2. When the nut is off, pull the flywheel with a puller (a device that screws into the two or three tapped holes on the flywheel and pulls the flywheel from the shaft as you turn it) or pry it off with two screwdrivers.

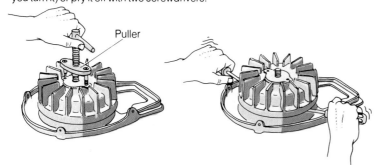

Puller

Checking the Breaker Points

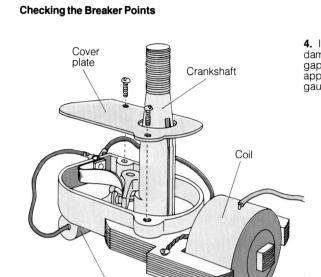

1. Remove the plate covering the breaker points.

2. Turn the crankshaft to open the points as far as possible. If they won't open, check the locking screw. If it's loose, tighten it. If it's tight and the points still won't open, replace them (see text).

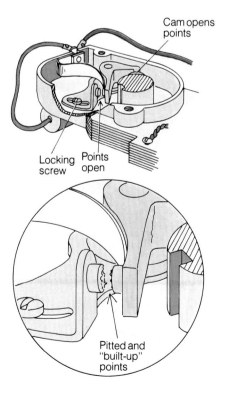

3. Check the points closely to see if they are damaged —burned, pitted, or have a metal "build-up." If they are damaged, replace them.

4. If the points aren't damaged, check the gap with the appropriate feeler gauge (see text).

5. To adjust the gap, loosen the locking screw, put the proper feeler gauge between the points, move the stationary point against the feeler, and tighten the screw. Some points have an adjustment screw that widens the gap when turned clockwise and narrows it when turned counter-clockwise. See the Maintenance Manual for your particular engine.

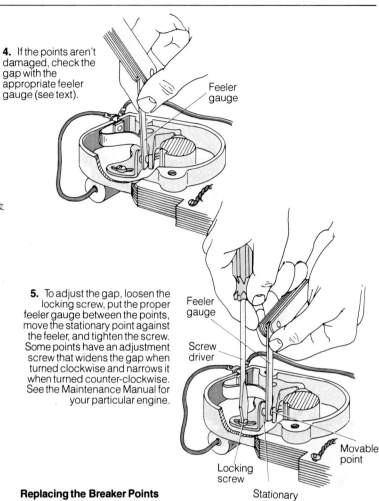

Replacing the Breaker Points

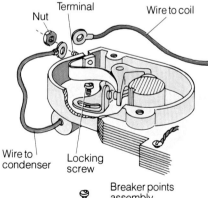

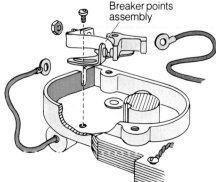

1. Remove locking screw and the nut on the wire terminal. Disengage the wires to the coil and condenser.

2. Lift out the point assembly and discard it.

3. Put the new points in place, attach the coil and condenser wires, insert the locking screw, and tighten it lightly.

4. Adjust the points with the proper feeler gauge (see drawing of "Checking the Breaker Points") and tighten the locking screw.

5. Put a dab of grease on the crankshaft to reduce wear on pusher arm or fiber block.

6. Replace the cover plate.

Basic Carburetor Adjustments

If your engine won't start or runs poorly, check all the other possibilities (see the trouble-shooting list on page 94) before you even think of fiddling with the carburetor. But if the problem is nowhere else, it may be in the carburetor—particularly if you have recently had it overhauled.

There are two basic adjustments you can make on the carburetor: You can adjust the idle speed or the flow of fuel.

The idle speed is regulated by a screw attached to the throttle linkage near the carburetor. To adjust the idle speed, simply turn the screw one way or another. This puts pressure on, or releases pressure from, the throttle. Tighten the screw to increase the idle speed, and loosen the screw to lower the idle speed. Make this adjustment when the engine is running and thoroughly warmed up.

Full-flow adjustment valves are controlled by one or more screws called needle valves. These screws have tapered tips to control the amount of fuel that flows into the carburetor. Tightening the screw moves the needle tip deeper into the valve and reduces the flow of fuel into the carburetor. The needle-valve screw is brass,

Idle Adjustment

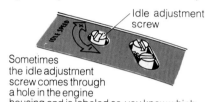

The idle speed of an engine can be adjusted with a screw, usually on the throttle lever on or near the carburetor. (**Note:** The actual appearance of these parts is different on each engine. See your own Maintenance Manual).

Sometimes the idle adjustment screw comes through a hole in the engine housing and is labeled so you know which way to turn it to slow or speed up the idle.

therefore soft, so never overtighten it.

Before you make an adjustment, note the precise location of the screw slot; if need be, you will be able to return the slot to that position. If you find that making an adjustment has not solved the problem,

return the screw slot to its original location.

To make the adjustment, let the engine run; turn the screw a quarter-turn to the right and listen for any change in the engine's sound. Now give the screw a quarter-turn to the left past the original position and compare the sound of the engine. If your problem is in the needle-valve adjustment, you should be able to find one particular position that will make the engine run faster and smoother. Turn the needle valve until the engine sounds best, and leave the valve there. If there is no position that will make the engine sound right, then the problem is not in the needle valve adjustment, and you should return the screw to the original position and check elsewhere for the problem.

If you have completely lost the original position of the screw, carefully tighten it all the way down and then back off one and a quarter turns. Start the engine and make small adjustments until the engine sounds best.

Some carburetors may have two needle valves side by side. The one closest to the source of air into the carburetor is for adjusting low speeds and idling. The other is for adjusting operating speeds.

Adjusting the Fuel Flow Adjustment Valves (Needle Valves)

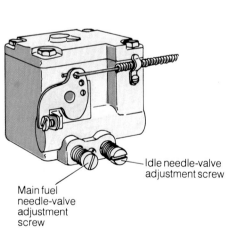

Main fuel needle-valve adjustment screw

Idle needle-valve adjustment screw

Look in your Owner's Manual or your Maintenance Manual to find the adjustment screws on your carburetor. They may be side by side, they may be on different sides, or they may protrude through the engine housing (especially on chainsaws).

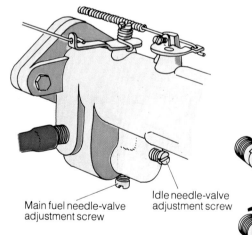

Main fuel needle-valve adjustment screw

Idle needle-valve adjustment screw

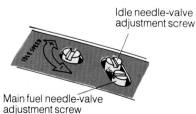

Idle needle-valve adjustment screw

Main fuel needle-valve adjustment screw

1. Study and note the precise position of the screw slot.

2. Rotate the screw ¼-turn to the right and listen for a change in the engine sound.

3. Rotate it back to the left ¼-turn past the original position and compare engine sounds (see text).

TOOLS FOR ENGINE MAINTENANCE

You don't need a warehouse full of mechanic's tools just to do standard engine-care. The tools listed here will do. They are not expensive, and if you do general work around the house and on appliances, the car, and small gas engines, you should own most of them.

Standard screwdrivers: You should have small, medium, and large sizes.

Phillips screwdrivers: Again, you need small, medium, and large sizes.

Adjustable wrench: The medium size (about 8 inches long) is good for a wide variety of work.

End wrenches: A set of these wrenches, with both open and closed ends, is vital for reaching into tight spots and is generally useful for many jobs.

Hammer: A 16-ounce, curved-claw hammer is best for general house and shop use.

Needle-nose pliers: These slim pliers allow you to work in tight places. Most have a wire-cutting edge near the pivot point.

Slip-joint pliers: These are useful for gripping hard-to-hold parts on an engine, and they adjust to two different sizes. However, do not substitute them for wrenches on nuts and bolts, which are easy to damage.

Socket wrench with sockets: This item costs a little more than a single tool, but it is well worth the price. The sockets slip over hard-to-reach nuts and give the socket wrench more gripping and turning power than an adjustable wrench.

Locking pliers: These are a cross between pliers and a wrench. They can grab and hold a nut that is otherwise impossible to turn. As with the slip-joint pliers, the locking pliers may damage the nut, but at least you'll be able to get it off and replace it.

Spark plug gauge: (see page 86).

Funnel: (see page 77).

Flywheel holder: (see page 90).

Flywheel puller: (see page 90).

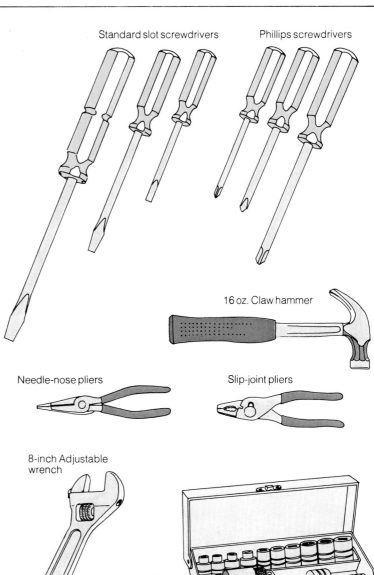

Standard slot screwdrivers

Phillips screwdrivers

16 oz. Claw hammer

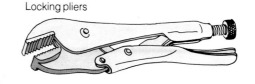

Needle-nose pliers

Slip-joint pliers

8-inch Adjustable wrench

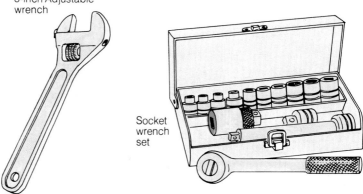

Socket wrench set

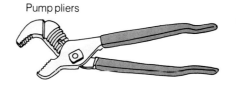

Locking pliers

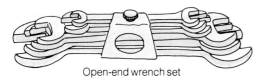

Open-end wrench set

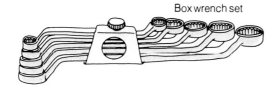

Box wrench set

Pump pliers

TROUBLE-SHOOTING THE SMALL ENGINE

When an engine won't start or runs poorly, here's what to look for:

If the Engine Is Hard to Start

1. The vent hole on top of the gas cap is plugged, creating a vacuum in the fuel tank. If the engine starts when the gas cap is removed, a plugged vent hole is the problem. Solution: Clean out the vent hole.

2. The air filter is clogged. Remove the air filter unit and try starting the engine. If it starts, clean and replace the filter.

3. The fuel line is partially plugged. Remove it and blow it out.

4. The spark plug is fouled. Remove and inspect it (see "Analyzing Spark Plugs," page 87). If the electrodes are worn or very dirty, replace the plug.

5. The spark plug wire is worn out. This wire carries high-voltage electricity from the coil, and any breaks in it may cause a loss of power or a short circuit. Wrap any breaks with electrician's tape or replace the wire.

6. The choke isn't operating properly. With a cold engine, the choke should close completely to make the fuel mixture richer. Remove the cover on the carburetor and inspect the choke in both the open and closed positions. Clean by spraying with carburetor solvent.

If you close the choke when starting a warm engine, the combustion chamber will have too much gas for ignition to occur. This is called "flooding" the engine. If you can smell gas when the engine won't start, let it rest 10 minutes and try again, this time with the choke open.

7. There is water in the gasoline. This is a common problem in an engine that has been stored with gas in the tank during the winter. Condensation collects and forms a puddle at the bottom of the tank. To remedy, drain the tank and fuel line and put in fresh gasoline.

8. The kill switch is malfunctioning. Engines are shut off with a kill switch that grounds all the electricity. If an engine won't fire at all, check to make sure that the kill switch is not accidentally closed. You can also remove the wire from the kill switch to check that the problem isn't in the wire itself.

9. The points are worn. If the problem can't be traced to any other cause, inspect the points and replace if necessary, as outlined on page 91.

Vented Gas Caps

Vent

Filtered vent on a chain saw

Damaged Spark Plug Wire

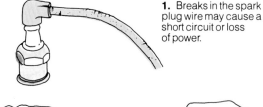

1. Breaks in the spark plug wire may cause a short circuit or loss of power.

2. Wrap minor damage to insulation with electrician's tape. If cracks are severe, replace the wire.

Checking the Choke

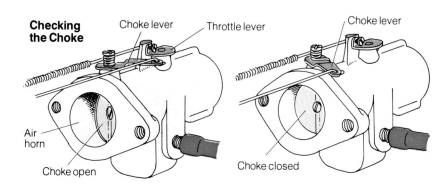

Choke lever

Throttle lever

Choke lever

Air horn

Choke open

Choke closed

1. Remove the carburetor cover or the air filter to get a good view of the choke.

2. Move the choke lever back and forth to see if the choke opens and closes completely.

3. As long as you have it exposed, clean the choke by spraying it with carburetor solvent.

Kill Switch

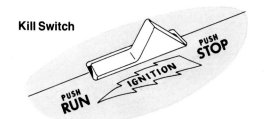

PUSH STOP

IGNITION

PUSH RUN

Somewhere near the throttle lever or trigger is the kill switch. This is one of many configurations.

If the Engine Performs Poorly

1. The air filter is clogged. Not enough air is reaching the carburetor to mix properly with the fuel. Remove the filter unit and see whether the engine's performance improves. If it does, clean and replace the filter.

2. The choke hasn't been opened after the engine is running. As the engine warms up, it needs more air for a leaner fuel mixture.

3. There's a clogged vent in the fuel cap. This causes a partial vacuum in the tank, which restricts the flow of gasoline. Remove the cap to see if this is the problem.

4. The fuel line is clogged. Remove and blow out the foreign material.

5. There's water in the gasoline. Gas that's been left in a tank for more than six months may collect condensation water. Drain the tank and fuel line and install fresh gasoline.

6. The carburetor is dirty. Remove the cover of the carburetor and look inside. Spray thoroughly with a carburetor solvent.

7. The carburetor is adjusted improperly. See information on carburetor needle valves in "Basic Carburetor Adjustments," page 92.

8. The engine won't reach normal speed. Check the linkage to the throttle. If the engine speeds up when you turn the throttle by hand, readjust the linkage.

9. The engine is running too hot. Check to make sure that the cooling fins around the engine are not filled with grass or other debris. If they aren't, then—if yours is a four-cycle engine—check the oil level. The oil should reach at least to the bottom part of the threads on the oil cap.

If the Engine Vibrates Excessively

1. The engine mounting bolts may be loose. Shut down the engine and check the bolts.

2. The cutting blade is out of balance. This is due to incorrect sharpening or a very large nick. See lawn mower section page 40.

3. There's a problem in the flywheel. This problem may be a worn retaining key, a cracked flywheel, or a broken flywheel tooth. Inspect and replace if necessary.

When to Take Your Engine to a Repair Shop

You can keep your engine out of the repair shop for years by doing the routine maintenance and tune-ups yourself. But when you need a major overhaul, you need to call in the professionals.

Some engine problems signal major overhauls. If your engine acts up in any of the following ways, take it to the pros:

☐ If the engine refuses to start, despite your best efforts.

☐ If the slot in the crankshaft that holds the retaining key for the flywheel has been enlarged through wear. A new crankshaft probably will be required. However, if only the key is worn, you can replace it yourself.

☐ If the breaker points are coated with oil. This indicates a leak in the oil seal.

☐ If the spark plug in a four-cycle engine is repeatedly coated with oil, causing the engine to consistently run poorly. This may indicate worn piston rings.

When you go to the repair shop, first get a good estimate of how much it will cost to have the repair work done. Compare that price against the cost of replacing the old engine with a factory-rebuilt engine.

Safety

Safety is a little like the weather: Everybody talks about it but nobody does much about it. But you need to get hurt only once to become safety conscious forever.

Basically, what's needed is common sense—in short, know what you are doing. Don't go into the woods with your trusty chainsaw and plan to saw a tree 5 feet in diameter unless you are experienced.

Safety also means planning ahead—that is, knowing ahead of time what the reaction will be to your action. When you swing an axe, make sure it hits where you aimed. If you cut down a tree, make sure it falls in the right direction.

Keep your working conditions neat. Clutter makes an accident a lot more likely to happen—tripping you up and causing general confusion by its mere presence.

Work slowly and methodically and always keep your balance. You're headed for trouble if you manhandle a rotary tiller around a turn or overreach for a branch with a chainsaw and lose your balance.

Good cultivation techniques are part of safety practices. Keep your hand relaxed when holding tools. Tighten your grip only when the tool touches earth or wood—a continuously firm grip will channel tension through your arms to your back and make you long for the easy chair. When possible, change hands to allow one side of your body periodic relaxation.

Safety Equipment

Wearing protective equipment is part of good safety practice. Depending on the kind of work you are doing, you might consider any or all of the following:

Gloves are designed to protect your hands from blisters, painful splinters, and cuts that can lead to infection. Leather gloves last a long time and protect well, but they aren't cheap; cotton work gloves cost less and also provide good protection. Use rubber or plastic disposable gloves when you work with chemicals such as those used for spraying plants and trees. If you are gloveless when working with a shovel or hoe, rub your hands with some dirt to keep them dry—moist hands blister easily.

Work Boots vary widely in cost, quality, and style. Choose what best suits your needs. You will probably need the extra protection of steel-toed boots if you are working with heavy materials or tools.

Safety Goggles are most useful when you are using a bench grinder to sharpen tools. The grinding process throws thousands of small metal fragments, seen as sparks, into the air. Just one of them can be painful and possibly damaging to your eyes. Also wear safety goggles when you use a splitting maul and steel wedge to split firewood. Wedges can chip and send a splinter of steel toward your eyes.

A Hard Hat is mandatory when working in the woods with a chainsaw. Dead limbs can and do fall out of trees. Loggers call these limbs "widow makers" for good reason.

Ear Protectors are suggested for anyone who does much work with a chainsaw—the noise of the engine can actually damage hearing. Use small rubber ear plugs or the earmuff-style protectors worn by target shooters. Either type will block out the ear-damaging sound of the engine but will still allow you to hear someone talking to you.

Dust Masks protect you when working in dusty conditions, such as when driving a small tractor in a garden or orchard. To some degree they will also filter out pollen in the air.

Respirators, however, do a much better job of filtering the air; you should definitely wear one if you do extensive spraying with pesticides. This is especially important when you direct the spray high in the air, as in an orchard. Respirators contain filters that screen out most of the toxic elements in pesticides. There are specific filters that will give maximum protection on specific pesticides. Consult the pesticide manufacturer for the best filter in each case.

INDEX